THE RACE

YEAR HISTORY OF THE
NING WALKING RACES
1903 – 2003

by

Ian Ivatt

Courtesy of Steyning Athletic Club

Published by Vernon Books Ltd., Steyning, 2003

Printed in Great Britain by Faulwood and Herbert, Brighton

ISBN 0-9546925-0-0

BY THE SAME AUTHOR

Lorna Binns – As I know her (Private) - 1999

Food For Thought – Wartime in Steyning   - 2000

A Steyning Connection - 2001

The Missing Satchel (with S. Skilton and A. Terry) - 2002

Steyning Conversations - 2002

CONTENTS

FOREWORD

I was honoured to be asked to write this foreword to The Race. My first recollections go back to the early 1930's when as a young boy the Easter Monday 15 Mile Race was one of the highlights of the year, when Small Dole would be crowded with onlookers. We would all watch to see Johnny Henderson go through. Little did I realise then that more than twenty five years later I would be taking part myself.

Ian has devoted great care in writing the history of The Race going back to the early days when a group of enthusiasts first conceived the idea of establishing this event and following through the years showing how the race organisation developed in such areas as finance and dress styles, together with the change of venue until the present club headquarters in Charlton Street. This has all gone to make Steyning Athletic Club one of the most famous names in Race Walking.

This book will appeal not only to the dedicated race walker, but also to anyone in the Steyning and surrounding areas, who is interested in local history. The town of Steyning is recognised by those fascinated with sport through such achievements such as Norman Read's 50 km Olympic Gold Medal and the other national and international honours held by the local Club Members.

This book illustrates that without the dedication of the backroom helpers, committee members, benefactors, fund raisers and all other organisers of the event, there would not have been any Race, and certainly without other competitors and "back markers" there would be no winners. I congratulate Ian on a very comprehensive study and may the Steyning Athletic Club survive for yet another one hundred years.

Tom Tidy,
Henfield, December 2003.

Tom has competed in the 15 mile event from 1957, and whilst he has never won the event, he has achieved many an excellent time. Furthermore Tom has appeared on twenty consecutive annual occasions in the Hastings to Brighton walk, and similarly on twenty consecutive occasions in the London to Brighton walk with three appearances in the London to Brighton and back again competition. He has achieved three separate 100 mile walks, each within a twenty four hour period. He holds the coveted title of Centurion – number 298.

ACKNOWLEDGEMENTS

I am grateful to Steyning Athletic Club for the comprehensive range of material, especially news cuttings and photographs, loaned to me for the purposes of this book. Also, I owe a debt of gratitude to my wife, Jacqueline for her ongoing help to complete this project, for checking the final manuscripts and suggesting corrections where required!

My sincere thanks must be recorded as due to Mary French, who spent countless hours, without complaint or demur to place these words and pictures into a sensible draft ready for printing. As usual, her contribution was invaluable.

Equally I am honoured that Walking Race veteran and Centurion Tom Tidy, has been kind enough to write the Foreword. His contribution to road walking, both locally and nationally, is far reaching, as are his experiences and memories. Tom, additionally, made available without question, his entire stock of past programmes, and other personal archival material, from which a sizeable amount of this narrative has been drawn.

SPECIAL THANKS ARE DUE TO:

The Adcock family members	Rev'd. Canon Peter Burch	Martin Sorrell
Betty Ash	Martin Coleman	Neil Sorrell
Lesley Ashby	Martin Ford-Dunn	Sarah Sowerby
Ivy Ashdown	Johnny Miller	Rose and Dave Stevens
George Barker	Cherry Neate	Darrell Stone
Charlie Bean	Doris Penfold	Douglas Tweed
Jeannie Bleach	Robert Rice	Mary Worth

ADDITIONAL ACKNOWLEDGEMENTS TO:

Mike Blackie	Mike Parker	Chris Tod (Steyning Museum)	Bob Webster
Colin Garlick	Dennis Read	Leonard Warner	

OTHER SOURCES:

Christ's Hospital Magazine (September 1977)
"Orders of the Day" re: Earl Winterton/Viscount Turnour, Cassell & Co., 1953
Southwick Evening Institute
"A Steyning Connection", I. J. V. Ivatt, Vernon Books, 2001
West Sussex County Times
County Registrars at Worthing and Brighton
West Sussex Records Office
Lewis Wood papers (from Club records and "Steyning Conversations", I. J. V. Ivatt, Vernon Books, 2002)

INTRODUCTION

The story of the Steyning Fifteen Mile Walking Race goes back one hundred years to the first such contest in 1903. Since that time, numerous changes to the format of this competition have been tried, tested, discarded, and on occasions, adopted. The information and detail garnered for this publication has been carefully preserved, mainly through the Race committee Minute Notebooks, but due regard has also been taken of press reports (where available), other archival sources and of equal, if not greater prominence, personal recollections. For the early years of the Race, memory recall, even odd artefacts produced, have been invaluable in adding specific social and historic credence to what might easily be considered merely as an account of an athletic event in an ordinary Sussex town.

Steyning has every right to be proud of the Walking Race, which (some might say, for this reason alone) undoubtedly sets it apart from similar sized towns. Perhaps it is the location, the lure of the South Downs and the countryside, or simply the foresight and fortitude of these individuals – contestants, organisers, supporters and spectators, who made it happen, that have contributed to the success – because this is what has been achieved – of this unusual race.

Fortunately, many Steyning families, (and special significance of this will be found in this work) who are still represented today, and all participants both young and old can remember with a large measure of pride, that they were involved and that an ongoing body of local Race Committee men and well wishers made it a memorable occasion.

The story in this book traces the race history, as stated from the beginning, although a sizeable slice of thanks must go to the Honourable (Minute) Secretaries' diligent recording techniques. Mr. Dennis West held this prestigious amateur post for many years, and he was, and no discredit to those before and after him, a great asset in the annals of local history.

This publication effectively follows the committee and later the Walking (Athletic) Club's progress, thematically, since 1903, (save for the first chapter which is intended to convey an overall picture) rather than relying on a chronological type of approach. The intention being to focus on the historic aspects of one emerging Steyning characteristic, albeit shaped around a race, that not only welded townspeople and sportsmen together – on one occasion, in 1956 to produce an Olympic Gold Medallist – but to serve as an example to us all as to what is achievable and what could actually be attained. I hope that other such towns, with or without a Race Walking connection, will be interested in the message in these pages.

Ian Ivatt,
Steyning, 2003.

AUTHOR'S NOTE

Money values, for example prize money awards or programme costs, are referred to, from time to time in the text, and for the avoidance of doubt are shown in the pounds, shillings and pence format prior to decimalisation, and pounds and pence thereafter.

To enable the reader to compare such amounts mentioned in any meaningful way, especially relevant for the earlier years of this study, the following table of average annual earnings for skilled men may serve as a useful guide:

1906	£97	
1924	£182	
1935	£197	
1955	£629	
1960	£804	
1978	£3701	(Average Clerk's pay)

Source: "*Occupation and Pay in Great Britain*" *1906 – 1979, by Guy Routh, Macmillan Press 1965.*

1 guinea =	£1.05p	(Decimal equivalent)
10 shillings =	£0.50p	(Decimal equivalent)
5 shillings =	£0.25p	(Decimal equivalent)
2/6d =	£0.12½p	(Decimal equivalent)

RULES OF RACE WALKING (IN BRIEF)

"The main requirement is that one foot must always be in contact with the ground. This can normally only be achieved by the lead foot making contact with the ground by means of the heel, whilst contact is maintained by the toe of the trailing foot. The more experienced walkers will also be judged on the straightness of the knee joint, as this determined the correct stance as the stride rate is increased. Walkers will be cautioned [by Judges], (or worse) if they are not abiding with the spirit of the sport".

Source: Steyning Athletic Club "Festival of Sport" brochure 2002

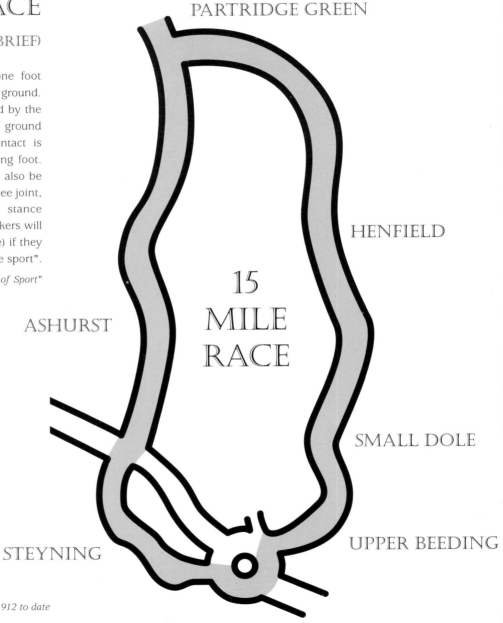

PARTRIDGE GREEN

HENFIELD

15 MILE RACE

ASHURST

SMALL DOLE

STEYNING

UPPER BEEDING

The course, first in 1903 and then from 1912 to date
Source: Steyning Athletics' Club.

GLOSSARY OF TERMS

Stewards, Marshalls, Judges, Timekeeper, Recorder, Starter

Race Officials.

Pivot Man

Race official stationed at the Fountain Inn signpost at Ashurst for the Juniors Race, from 1925. Position later moved to Horsebridge Common.

Collector

Committee Member who collected donations, vouchers, and programme sale money.

Balance Sheet

Annual Accounts.

Smoking Concert

Post Race Day entertainment.

Tradesman's Vouchers

Part of prize system, such vouchers were distributed to the race winners (and losers).

The Committee

Walking Race Committee, formal meeting minutes date from 1912 until 1938.

Handicap or Sealed Handicap System

The standard method of adjusting a walker's finishing time by reference to age and experience, to create a better opportunity of prize winning.

Flag Man

Particular Race Official pre Second World War.

A.A.A.

Amateur Athletic Association.

Lifting

Illegal walking action.

Rules of Walking or Walking Rules (effectively modern interpretation)

Rules governing the Race itself and method of accepted "walking".

Centurion

Walker who has completed 100 miles in a continuous 24 hour period.

CHAPTER ONE

HOW IT ALL BEGAN.
AN OVERVIEW OF THE EARLY YEARS, 1903 ~ 1923

Race Walking, for hundreds of years known as Pedestrianism is steeped in history. Centuries ago, wagers would be made on whether or not men such as George Cummings could walk between two particular village pubs within the hour. George was also credited with walking between London and York in 73 hours, 11 hours faster than a racehorse. During the 18th and 19th centuries, pedestrians such as Robert Bartley frequently walked the 81 miles from Thetford in Norfolk to London returning home on foot the following day. In 1806, 62 year old Joseph Edge from Macclesfield won 200 guineas by covering a distance of 83 miles in less than 24 hours beating a younger Captain Hewetson in the process. Robert Allardice born in 1779 became one of the best known pedestrians and has been credited with many exploits. Starting on 1st June 1809, he walked 1000 miles in 1000 consecutive hours on Newmarket Heath. This remarkable feat was surpassed by that of Josiah Eaton who at the age of 45 walked 1100 miles in 1100 successive hours.

Source: Easter Monday Walking Race Brochure, 1994.

As far as Steyning is concerned, the precise origin of the "Easter Monday Walking Races" can be found in the Norfolk Arms Public House, in Church Street. Members of the elite "Ping Pong Club" were urgently debating not the great issues of the day such as Free Trade or the aftermath of the Boer War but the outcome of the 1903 Stock Exchange London to Brighton walking race. Individual wagers as to who might be the club's fastest walker then followed. What better way of proving or disproving the point then, by staging a local race by way of comparison. The fifteen mile road walking race was thereby born – starting and finishing in Steyning and going through the nearby villages of Ashurst, Partridge Green, Shermanbury, and Henfield.

Thus, on 6th May 1903, fifteen walkers started off with Horace Green finishing the course in a splendid 2 hours 40 minutes. Road surfaces, in 1903, were quite unlike those one hundred years later.

For the next eight years, various alternative fifteen mile courses were used but in 1912, the Race Walking Committee, under the Chairmanship of Major L. Colledge, later retiring in favour of Mr. Harry Oliver, decided to revert to the 1903 route. Interestingly enough, the Committee Members of that group still include family names in the town, both recently and today – Chalcraft, Wood, Burt, and Breach, together with a (presumed) German, Herr Von Zur Mullen! In addition to the usual formal committee appointments, the committee recommended some basic rules to govern the race in the future. According to the meeting minutes of 26 September 1912, these were held at Steyning Town Hall.

1. Persons residing within the limit of a radius of three miles from the Steyning Town Clock (of which more will be heard of later) shall be eligible to compete.
2. Each year the Race will take place on Easter Monday.
3. There will be a 2 o'clock start.
4. There shall be twenty persons appointed, to supplement the Chairman, Treasurer, and Secretary, to serve on the race committee.
5. The rules governing the actual race walking were as heretofore. *(Not described!)* A Silver Challenge cup was provided for the first man home.

The "rules" will be revisited in a later chapter and since 1912 have not sizeably varied.

Walkers in the first race of 1903. The winner Horace Green is seated on the ground, far left. Some in this race went on to compete in later years. Note "boot type" race footwear.

In these early days, the question of the cost of putting on the race was of paramount importance. The 1912 minutes record that at one stage three shillings was spent on programme printing with the Annual General Meeting (A.G.M.) expenses at the Town Hall incurring seven shillings and sixpence, to leave a whisker over three shillings in the Committee's petty cash fund!

The five guineas received from the "entertainment" that year, thereby placed the Committee's funds on a more respectable basis!

In that year of 1912, Ernie Adcock (1885 – 1977) romped home in 2 hours 22 minutes, 45 seconds. He was to repeat his success in the following year and in 1922 but in not quite such an excellent time. That record stood until 1929 when an emerging Johnny Henderson shaved off 38 seconds.

Despite individual subscriptions coming in, including a small donation from Steyning Breweries (arguably to recognise the post race level of uplifted ale consumption) and proposals for a new "Winners" cup, with cash prizes (ranging from £2.10 shillings to 15 shillings), up to the fifth best fastest time, cash flow consideration persisted into 1913. Nevertheless, subscriptions were still buoyant, now supplemented by local Tradesman's vouchers, to add to the prize monies. The profits from the "Smoker concert" that year also helped. However, leaving aside one outstanding item of expenditure on official's armbands, the committee found themselves in a position of some financial embarrassment during the 1913 A.G.M. at the George Public House, as the Secretary revealed "a balance of a few shillings on the wrong side". Committee members dug deep into their pockets by way of a financial rescue operation!

A surprise motion at the meeting suggested a change of headquarters venue from the George Inn to the Parish Room, but was marginally defeated. There was, however, an undercurrent of feeling for a change of venue.

The net "Christie Minstrels Concert" entertainment proceeds for 1914 amounting to £4. 5 shillings, made an excellent contribution to the Committee finances that year. Added to this were the repeat private subscriptions, including 10 shillings from another Teutonic admirer, Baron Von Muples, and an increased level of trade vouchers, supplied by W. Gray and Co., Messrs. Stone, Wood, Chapman, Stubbings and Bateman, C. W. Beck and Co., ranging from 7 shillings and sixpence to 5 shillings. A silver mounted walking stick and a pipe in a case were also donated as potential prizes. Steyning Brewery also added the customary 10 shillings.

Chairman Harry Oliver, President Major Colledge, and the entire committee looked forward, with the expanding list of participants, to an excellent Race Day of 6 April 1914, advertised in advance by posters and window bills. Just for the sake of completeness, competitors would be asked to fill in a form showing performances achieved at previous races to aid the complicated handicap (sealed) system to be applied. A separate new cup would be awarded for the fastest time, under handicap provisions, later known as the "Angus" Silver Challenge Cup. The organising aspects had clearly moved creditably forward, the event now being designated as the Steyning Annual 15 Mile Handicap Walking Race. Economically, too, the funding towards the end of that year took a turn for the better, being in credit by over two pounds!

Walkers in the 1914 Race, won by T. Terry in 2 hours 26 minutes – note the following cyclists, and early motor vehicles.

No races were held, nor indeed do official Committee Meeting Minutes exist, during the years 1915 – 1919, owing to the Great War.

There was evident enthusiasm to recommence the Race in the post war era and the first Committee Meeting occurred on 10 February 1920. Much had been learnt by the enforced wartime break of the Races, and in the questioning mode of the 1920's, changes to the existing format were proposed. Mr. Reginald Bateman was elected as Chairman with Colonel E. Suckling of Bayards as President. Vice Presidents duly elected now bore the names of many local worthies, Harry James Burt, Bernard Samuelson, Mitchell Breach, Colonel Young, Frank Duke, Charles Goring, and Dr. Wheeler Bennett amongst them. Two separate groups emerged favouring or otherwise a new headquarters for the Committee. Upon a vote, a majority now preferred the Chequers Hotel, which was to remain as the Committee's meeting point until well after the end of the next war. The Landlord of the George Inn was to be sent a vote of thanks, accordingly.

Moreover, it was successfully suggested that the catchment area for eligibility, set in 1912, be expanded to include residents of Ashurst, Wiston, Bramber, Beeding, Beeding Cement Works, and Small Dole. Separately there was a faction in the Committee that wanted to remove the starting and finishing points to the Steyning Cricket Field – the majority view of retaining the Steyning town clock for this purpose prevailed.

Subscription income, again Steyning Brewery provided 10 shillings, showed an increase as did the "Prizes in Kind" – Tradesman's vouchers grew larger, with additions from Burdocks, Cherryman, Ing, Earle, Rice, Hall and Joyes. Expenses, as anticipated were greater, now burdened by higher insurance premiums, including arrears from 1914, extensive poster costs, better winners prizes; 1st Place now three pounds ten shillings and programme expenditure priced at tuppence.

Ambulance costs are recorded, for the first time, set at fifteen shillings including drinks. Competitors too, helped, as a one shilling entry fee was established.

A balance of income over expenditure was achieved by additional funds raised in Whist Drive (net proceeds over £3) and by the benefit offered by the Sussex Electric Cinema Circuit (raised over £5) to result in a net overall surplus of income over expenditure for the year of nearly £5. This included money raised from collecting boxes in Steyning. George Holden, out of the 30 entries, won the 15 Mile Race that year, in a shade over 2 hours 29 minutes – he won four times in six races, to 1925.

No new provisions were proposed for the 1921 race, programmes, entrance fees, and prize money remaining unaltered. The Town Clock start and finish were endorsed by the local Police Superintendent. As it transpired the 15 mile race winner George Holden won the Open Challenge Cup outright, which meant a new cup, for next year was required. Subscription receipts, box collections, and donations held steady, as did outgoings. The cash balance in hand for that year was a little under £4 (as per Balance Sheet 1921 – and list of subscribers) the Cinema Entertainment effectively reflecting that year's surplus.

The 1922 Race was held under the same conditions and rules, excepting that the race was now open – otherwise a scratch contest. A new silver cup was introduced for the fastest time and presented by a Mr. Beesely. Committee changes were noteworthy. Mr. Fred Gander replaced Colonel Suckling as President, and the eminently reliable Dennis West became Honourable Committee

Secretary – a position he was to hold until 1946. With his appointment came the opening of the "Steyning Annual Walking and Race Committee" bank account with Lloyds Bank, Steyning Branch in April 1922. Matters moved up another gear when 400 programmes were ordered from the printers and the race participants had an official "dressing room", hired from a Mrs. Millward, at a cost of 7 shillings and sixpence! An identical expense was incurred for the Course Marshall's (Mr. S. Earl) pony and trap!

Rudimentary medical facilities were again on hand with the ambulance wagon. Financially, the year was a success with a credit cash surplus of nearly nine pounds, a whist drive, and box collections included. There were, however, the initial murmurings of racing under the auspices of the Amateur Athletic Association, so that Steyning Walkers could compete in walking races outside Steyning, but the matter was shelved for a future year – only to resurface later.

The Race Winner, out of twenty six entries, was Ernie Adcock, attaining 2 hours 29 minutes. Separately, a new prize "The Sexton Cup" was donated for the best Novice time to make three cup prizes. C. Pelling was the first such winner.

One of Ernie's fondest memories (of which there are many!) goes back to the turn of the 20th Century - in his own words:

"In the old days there were galleries each side of the [Steyning] *church and the services were packed. I remember, especially when we had the funeral services for Queen Victoria* [1901] *and Edward VII* [1910] *that boarders from Steyning Grammar School sat in oak pews up the centre aisle. These pews were made by our Churchwarden's grandfather, a Mr. Rapley."*

Source: Mrs. Hazel Mundell and Southwick Evening Institute "All our own work" 1970.

Adcock's walking record time stood for 17 years.

Ernest Albert Adcock 1885 – 1977. Although born in Hampshire, Ernie lived in Steyning from 1892. He had been a soldier, gardener, Special Constable and Church Verger in his time.

Additionally Griggs the Grocer and International Stores joined the ever growing list of subscribers, together with staff at Steyning Railway Station, with a guinea from Captain Purchas and a half guinea from the Honourable Claude Hamilton-Russell. Subscriptions and donations amounted to over £26 as compared with the £18 odd for 1921. A greater level of interest was now in evidence.

The 1924 Race Committee, chaired by G. J. Breach, made two specific decisions for that year, namely that any question of affiliation to the A.A.A. be dropped entirely and that no boys under the age of 16 were allowed to enter. The 1923 Course Marshall proposed that a girls walking race be held, commencing at 2.30 p.m. but the Committee ruled that they "would not support any other event held on the same day". Female participation, although raised again, would have to wait another 50 years and more.

The competition was well advertised that year with 50 race posters being printed and 27 entries were received, still at one shilling each. The event's popularity was becoming more widespread and local press news cuttings in the records reported that over 5000 people watched the event along the route as a whole. The Steyning Town Band added loyal support by playing between the 2 o'clock start and when the walkers safely returned.

For this year, the prizes value was in excess of £30, the faithful and growing list of subscribers playing their part in the underlying economy of the race representing over 50% of the total receipts. The whist drive also contributed £6. 7 shillings that, according to the balance sheet, helped to make a final "credit at the bank" for that year of a little over £5. The Committee Secretary thanked Steyning Police were their crowd control work. George Holden achieved his third fastest time victory in that year, and a £4 winner's prize voucher, whilst A. Mitchell took the "Angus" Silver Challenge Cup for the first Steyning man winning the "sealed handicap" contest, and a £2 voucher. The novices' "Sexton" Silver Challenge Cup went to E. Emsley, who went on to dominate the race 1924 and 1926 – 1928, with a £1. 5 shilling voucher.

A special point was made in the official programme warning cyclists, accompanying the walkers (which has already been noted, was the practice in these early years) not to "fall in" with the racing walkers until after Bayards House, at the Steyning boundary.

Official Programme, front page, price 2d, for the 1923 Easter Monday Walking Races. The front page logo of two men racing was to be unchanged until 1988.

CHAPTER TWO

THE ELIGIBILITY FACTOR, RACE OFFICIALS, AND THE COURSE ROUTE

With the race now firmly established, not only as a financially viable event, but as a keenly supported spectator occasion and with an experienced administrative system in the background, the way ahead was clear for the walkers to concentrate on achieving better time results. Adcock's 1912 time of 2 hours 22 minutes 45 seconds was still the record, but this was to be broken in 1929 and was consistently bettered thereafter. Under two hours was a target, but whilst nearly being cleared barring two seconds in 1958, was not seriously threatened until the 1970's, being finally surpassed in 1978.

Nevertheless, whilst nationally the 1920's and 1930's portrayed difficult average living standards, the Steyning Easter Monday Races seemed set on an upward climb. Perhaps it was due to the healthy country diet, or even an increased concept of the value of exercise; possibly as 86 year old Douglas Tweed, who took part in, and won, the boy's races 1928 and 1929, recalls, "conceivably all down to a better type of canvas shoe" – it might be all of these, and more.

Whilst there was a proposal to reduce the course down to 10 miles, this was pushed aside to leave the 15 miles, as in the past.

The last five years of the 1920's heralded changes, some quite far reaching. Dr. G. Wheeler-Bennett was asked to accept the Presidency, which he happily did and continued in his post from 1925 until 1931.

As we have seen in the previous chapter, basic eligibility rules had been established all supported by a Race Walking Committee who invariably, were collectively responsible for ensuring the finances were in order and on the Easter Monday the same Committee men, with outside help where appropriate, doubled up as Race Officials.

The 15 Mile Race Walking course was now well known and remains the same today. Similarly, those who could compete were only permitted to do so if in accordance with the 1912 definition. Some clarification was promised after the 1929 Races, prompted by a Committee residential ruling requirement for one walker, a Mr. Burr. As it was from 1928 the start and finish was altered to outside the Chequer Inn, as opposed to the Town Clock position. However, another issue arose prior to that in 1925 namely the question of Junior Race Walking – to reverse the 1924 decision of not allowing anyone under sixteen years of age to Race.

After due deliberation, the committee conceded to pressure to hold a 7 mile Junior Race for those aged between 12 and 16. The same residential qualification would apply, although the course was reduced to Ashurst and back to Steyning. The Fountain Inn signpost was the precise half way mark. The Juniors' entrance fee was fixed at 6d.

Chairman G. J. Breach and his faithful 1925 committee set a £20 prize allotment figure, split between the first six fastest walkers, three handicap awards and, similarly three for the Novices; all ranging from £4 to 10 shillings. Moreover, £9 was provided for the Juniors, shared between the six fastest walkers, and six handicap prizes. The £2 winners cash was a handsome sum in 1925, for a boy. To help this extra expense, yet another successful Whist Drive and Dance was held although additional costs were incurred for polishing the floor (three shillings) and providing a conveyance for the Band at £1. Donations were buoyant even sizeably better that year. Both Harry Joyes and the President presented new cups that year.

Seventeen Juniors set off at 11 o'clock for Ashurst, followed by eighteen for the 15 mile walk at 2 o'clock. G. Holden romped home in a time of 2 hours 27 minutes 18 seconds to extend his own record whilst J. Manvell had arrived back first for the Juniors in just over 1 hour 6 minutes.

Yet Adcock's record 2 hours 22 minutes 45 seconds of 1912 had still to be broken.

Financially it was another success, as with the extra box collections during the race, sufficient money had been obtained, to give the Steyning Town Band and the Sussex County Hospital a decent guinea each.

First Juniors' Race 1925 (intriguing variety of styles!)

On the occasion of the first committee meeting of 1926, it was decided to also offer "Boys' Races", for those lads under twelve. The difficulty was – which course should be chosen? Finally, by 17 votes to 5, a course starting at the Town Clock in the High Street was selected, via the Dairy, Castle Lane, Goring Road, Cripps Lane and back to the Town Clock.

Thus, both the Juniors and the Boys starts in 1928 were from the Town Clock position, although, by the Committee's approval, the Juniors course was shortened to Spithandle Lane, Horsebridge Common and back, rather than to the Fountain Inn at Ashurst and return. Ernie Tellick volunteered as "Pivot Man" (see Glossary of Terms). Boys only paid 3d as opposed to the previous 6d to enter from 1927. In these economically difficult years, the races went smoothly enough, money to run the event was raised – thanks to wise committees, the "Shoreham Follies" concert profits, and Whist Drive money, to balance the books. Turnover in the years 1926, 1927 and 1928 was £58, £51 and £64 respectively, outgoings just falling short of the total receipts to leave a small balance every time. This was sufficient to even make small donations to local hospitals and the Town Band.

Ominously for the other walkers, a twenty two year old John Henderson made his mark, third fastest time at 2 hours 32 minutes 53 seconds – a time he would easily surpass by winning six of the next eight annual 15 Mile races in the years 1929 – 1936.

The entire town was now becoming increasingly involved – the Fire Brigade supplying crowd control ropes, First Aid Car provided by Mr. Arthur Rodda, lengthening lists of cash subscribers – including the Steyning Brewery, Griggs Grocers, International Stores, the Goring's, Reverend Cox and many others – printers and advertising also played its part, programme sales, insurances and the Dressing Rooms courtesy of Mrs. Casey again.

The next year 1929 would reflect another change of emphasis and a farcical brush with politics (See Chapter 5).

The year 1930 brought the promised rule reviews, in the wake of the Burr case, focussing on the eligibility aspect. In brief: -

1. Only entrants, by birth or residence from Steyning, Wiston, Ashurst, Bramber, Beeding, Small Dole and the "cement works" could compete.

2. Residence to mean, 30 days immediately prior to the race or for a previous period of one year.

3. If any cup holder permanently left the areas as in Rule 1, the cup must be returned to the Secretary.

Start of 1928 15 Mile Handicap Race from outside the Chequer Inn. The legendary Johnny Henderson is wearing number 8.

The Committee retained the services of all its constituent members, and no other changes in Race matters were suggested, save for a varied Junior course, now to be re-routed to Bramber, Beeding, Sele, and back. A dance and whist drive were to create the funds, which resulted at an overall profit for the entire event of over £3 in the 1930 Balance Sheet figures. In the fifteen mile event, J. F. Chandler took the honours that year in a new record time of 2 hours 21 minutes 7 seconds, and also scooped four cups for himself in the process. Thirty walkers are recorded on the Race programme for that year, with 12 Juniors and 14 Boys.

Prize money and tradesman's vouchers were distributed as usual, and unplaced boys were each awarded a consolation prize of one shilling. At the final committee meeting that year, another four guinea honorarium was voted to the Honourable Secretary. The Police, Judges, and other officials were all thanked. A recommendation was also made as to the advisability of having iodine and bandages on hand in the Dressing Room for future Races.

By this time, Race officials were imposing a firm but fair grip on the proceedings and in a later chapter, the subsequent issue of the Amateur Athletic Association's involvement – leading to an uplifted "club" status will be examined.

A number of "Stewards" and later "Marshalls", were appointed for each race with starters and separate judges all officiating in the three distinct classes; Seniors, Juniors and Boys. A Timekeeper, sometimes there were two, was appointed and at the finish a "man at the tape" was stationed. In these early years of Race Walking the Marshalls undertook the same task as required in 2003, namely to ensure walkers kept to the correct method of walking, thus avoiding disqualification or at least an initial warning; for lifting. Printed on the programmes of the 1920's and 1930's was the Race Walking Committee's appeal to retain a "sportsmanlike spirit" and requested that the Stewards orders "be complied with". It is essentially the same in the 21st Century.

The start of the Boys Race, from the Town Clock, 1929. All under 12 years of age, including such names as Boyd, Shepherd, Standing, Charman, Tweed, Dumbrell, Henley, Williams, Pitness, and Parsons.

10.30 a.m. Start, from Steyning Town Clock, of Juniors Race 1931. It was exceptionally wet that year, but partially cleared for the afternoon Seniors' 15 Mile event. The Juniors route went through Bramber, Beeding, Sele Gardens and Court, the Rising Sun and back to Steyning High Street. The starter Bertram Nicholls is standing on the left. Note the beginnings of ladies shorter skirt fashion. Almost all the men are wearing a cap or hat.

CHAPTER THREE

SUPPORTERS, HELPERS AND RACE FOLLOWERS

As has been seen and, indeed, will be expanded upon in the chapter relating to newspaper coverage, the Steyning Easter Monday Races provided entertainment on the day almost achieving near cult status. If there was no governing committee aided by the officials, the races would simply not happen – yet coupled with the ever growing band of volunteer helpers and supporters, it did take place, in a unique manner. Race followers added richness to an already exciting local spectacle.

One keen supporter was Colin Garlick, born in 1924 in the Chequer Public House in Steyning High Street. Colin's claim that the Chequer Inn was, in the 1950's and later, the focal centre of village life, and that the races created supreme local interest, was well founded. He should know, as he was the licensee there, with his wife Norma, from 1948 until 1990. Colin well remembers Easter Mondays as it turned out to be the busiest trading day of the year, both before and after the Races. He opened all day and many people, including families, came in to the Inn, some of whom he never saw for the rest of the year! Colin's main recollection was of letting the Senior Race competitors use the Inn's bathroom, lodge room – even Colin's bedroom as changing room facilities – and in particular of athletes rubbing liniment on their limbs. The resultant smell of the stuff, he adds, took up to two weeks to disappear! The Chequer Inn front window was, from 1932, used to display the Handicap results of the 15 mile event.

Former Steyning Grammar School boy Robert Rice gives his view of the Race day, as a helper and spectator. Robert now runs an antique business in Malvern, Worcestershire.

"*I only got involved in the races as a marker, programme seller and general assistant – that being in my capacity as a member of 1st Steyning Scouts. There were around two dozen of us. Easter Monday was the first day of bob-a-job week when able lads like myself touted for work to add to scout funds without fear or even thought of molestation. How times have changed.*

The whole town turned out to enjoy the competitions, the 1 mile, 3 mile, and 7 mile in the morning and the 15 mile in the afternoon. The High Street was always packed, regardless of the weather. Neither competitors nor onlookers were deterred by rarely heat, frequently rain and often snow – the greenhouse effect had not been invented then, although it had been suggested that the Gulf Stream was changing direction and that was why the 1950's were so cold and wet.

There were a couple of ambulances to hand, but the odd collapse was treated with a glass of water and a lift back to the High Street by either a mate or the police. Cycle support was generally not considered necessary for the morning events but dozens of us used to cycle the 15 mile course rain, shine, or snow. I have no notion of how many times I followed the race, but we always had to make it to the clock tower to see the leader come in."

Local resident, Doris Penfold, who came to Steyning at the age of eight with her family in 1925 specifically recollects watching the races in those pre World War Two days, with her sister Rene; both sisters sporting new hats and dresses specially made for Easter by their mother. The two girls stood at George's Corner at the bottom end of the High Street, cheering on the walkers as they went by. Doris and Arthur's son, Ronald Penfold won the fifteen mile event in 1969 in the excellent time, (the best since 1958 when Norman Read, 1956 Olympic Gold Medallist of whom more will be told in the later chapter of The Record Breakers), of 2 hours 3 minutes, 24 seconds. In the 1970's Doris became a Race Committee member and was pleased enough to help on the Race Day to make the teas and sandwiches, eagerly consumed by the much fatigued fifteen milers on their return!

Another ex-Grammar School boy, Martin Sorrell, now Professor of Modern Languages at Exeter University has his own personal memories, albeit a little uncertain as regards the route.

"*I do have vague memories of the Easter Walking Races. I took part probably twice, but as a young boy, and only in the short one-mile race, which, I believe, was the first on the programme of events. I seem to remember a longer one then, the big 15 mile Classic. That one was dominated by the Steyning Athletic Club (to which I belonged, briefly), and I think there was an "oldie" called Henderson who always did well. As for me, I fought hard to finish somewhere in the middle. I suspect there were 20 or 30 entrants.*

It was exciting to be in those races in the early 50's. The build-up was considerable, as those races were a huge part of local mythology. My family came to see me, and I rather think my younger brother took part too at some stage. Whether I won some token prize, I can't remember. Nor can I exactly recall the route, except that we started by the clock tower, went down the hill probably past the Penny Drink shop, and on somewhere, was it Shooting Field? Eventually to Goring Road or was it up round the hill and down again? I'm sorry I just can't remember. My recollection is that it did not rain when I took part. In fact, in my mind it is always quite sunny weather, if fresh."

Another resident, born here in Steyning in 1919 is Mrs. Ivy Ashdown whose brothers, the Boyd's (also featuring in the "Threesomes" chapter) all participated in the Easter Monday Races. Ivy, known locally as "Fido" was educated at the National School in Steyning but later went on to a scholarship at Worthing High School for Girls. Fido's story, reproduced below, mirror images other testimonies of the Race Day occasion, and emphasises the family nature of the event.

"*There was always an increased amount of activity in our house every Easter Monday, centred mainly on the Walking Races. After watching the morning races, we had an early lunch because Auntie Violet, my mother's sister from Lancing, and Uncle Fred arrived on the 2.00 pm. bus to watch the 15 Mile race. Three of my brothers, Tim, Fred and Ted participated in this event and would meet at home to make the last minute preparations, such as packing the heels of their shoes with cotton wool or other substances to prevent blisters. My part was to accompany them round the course on my bicycle. Drink had to be prepared, water or soft drinks and I seem to remember we used glucose instead of sugar to sustain their energy. Competitors were not allowed to take any refreshments until they had progressed to Ashurst and I usually escorted them from Bayards onwards. Cycling at walking pace was somewhat arduous, and I have known rain, snow and on one occasion sun, which was so hot it caused sunburn. The worst part of the Race was from Small Dole onwards – uphill for most of the way, flagging spirits, tired legs, but determination got them to finish. My brothers would always like to finish as they started, the three of them together, although Ted would invariably push either Tim or Fred over the line in order for them to say they had beaten him. Each year spectators would look out for 'The Brothers' all the way around the course. Until a few years ago my nephew – Brian Boyd – (Ted's son) came down from Walsall to walk in the race, but by then myself and bicycle were not needed, but I still waited until 5.00 p.m. for him to finish. Easter Monday in my family was always Walking Race Day – sadly there is no-one left in my family who is able to carry on this tradition, but thankfully there are a lot of dedicated people who work so hard to keep these Races going.*"

Douglas Tweed, born in Ashurst in 1917, spent some of his younger days in nearby Lancing on the coast, but on returning to Steyning took part in both the 1928 and 1929 (second and third) "Boys" race, as an under 12 year old. He won on both occasions, scooping the fifteen shilling prize each time! Doug had to train for the race after he had helped with the chores on the family farm. His winning time in 1925 was 13 minutes, in 1929 13 minutes 23 seconds. On other years, he watched the races but Doug discontinued active participation in races after the death of his father.

Boys Race 1929, D. Tweed (winner) No. 8, E. Boyd (third place) – one of "Fido" Ashdown's brothers, no. 1. The changing room for Boys and Juniors was at Steyning Fire Station, in the High Street. Bertram Nicholls, the local well known artist, was the official starter for the Boys Races in both 1928 and 1929.

It was common practice to follow the afternoon Seniors Walking Race by bicycle. We have seen comment about this aspect already and the Race Walking Committee needed to remind the enthusiastic two wheeled supporters to keep their distance – printed on all the pre 1939 programmes. Special rules were keenly enforced to make cycling attendees at least 10 yards behind any walker.

The following pictures give an idea of the bicycle support during the Race, and also provide an insight into the clothing fashions of 1911, especially hats, plus the motor cavalcade of spectators in 1947.

1911 Race (Walker George "Carrots" Holden).

Last but by no means least in this chapter, a contribution from another former President, Mrs. Betty Ash, who tells her own personal story. Betty, as she is known to thousands, ran the specialist tobacco and sweet shop in Steyning for fifty years, retiring in 2002. Betty was born at the rear of the family shop in the High Street, and her father Frank Stubbings ran the cycle shop for many years – an aspect that Betty refers to in her narrative.

"My memories of Steyning Walking Races go back many years. My father, having been a founder member of the Races, always observed Easter Monday as 'Race Day' – so my Mother and I were also drawn into it. It started at about 8.30 a.m. with coils and coils of thick rope being carried up the street (we housed it during the year in our garden shed) this was laid down the street from the car park to Church Street on both sides of the road. 'What for?' you might ask – to hold the crowds back, yes, crowds. When the races were in progress it was nothing for the people to stand five and six deep on the pavements – so, if they trespassed onto the road, an 'Official' would give a short tug on the rope and it would soon pull you back. Besides the crowds, every window with a vantage point would be occupied. Oh! to see those numbers of spectators again. Incidentally, my father was not an athlete; his only claim to fame was a Sussex Senior Cup football medal for when he played for Shoreham (pre the First World War).

Pre the Second World War, having the Cycle Shop, he hired out bicycles for the locals to follow the walkers round the 15 mile course in the afternoon. I think the rental was five pence. Father was really 'chuffed' when asked to be the Club President; and, incidentally, so was I in more recent years."

Source, Steyning Athletics Club "Festival of Sport" brochure 2002.

Betty has also generously supported the Easter Monday races by supplying chocolate Easter Eggs for entrants to the children's race in the morning. For more details of Betty Ash's life – see "Steyning Conversations" by Ian Ivatt, Vernon Books, Steyning, 2002.

1947 Race (Walker, Johnny Henderson, no. 6).

CHAPTER FOUR

THE BALANCE SHEET

As has already been shown a "Race Walking Committee" was effectively responsible for running the Easter Monday races up to the early 1950's when the official "club" structure was implemented (see Chapter Nine). Part of the usual and annual administrative duties fell to the Treasurer and his assistant during these first fifty years (and so is the case today with even more complicated routines) to be summarised in the year end financial statement, now spoken of as the "annual accounts" but almost as a reminder of late Victorian and Edwardian language values referred to then, as the "Balance Sheet". It should be emphasized that without all this procedural yet steady background work, the Races would not have taken place at all.

In Chapter One, we have an overview of the early years of Race Walking, which includes references to the all important finances, which underpinned the entire venture. The Race Treasurer(s) relied on Race entrance fees, subscriptions from local sources, the kindness of local tradesmen and business people who supplied winners' vouchers, income from programme sales and profits from any Pre or Post Race "entertainment". The Treasurer's right hand man was any assistant that volunteered, as was the Walking Race Collector (see Glossary of Terms). Notable Treasurers in the period were Messrs. Worsfold, Bateman, Emsley, and Holmes with Ernie Adcock taking on yet another task as "Assistant Honourable Secretary".

A copy of the first ever Race Committee's Lloyds Bank account application of 10 April 1922 – signed by the Chairman, (G. J. Breach), Treasurer (R. Bateman), with the Secretary (D. West) also mentioned.

Additionally, there were a further 23 subscriptions of 5 shillings, 18 of two shillings and sixpence with 22 trade voucher prizes, 5 shillings in value to 15 shillings donated by Steyning businessmen.

Subscriptions to support the race, mainly from private individuals, with a small number of businesses (some years, additionally, a brewery also made donations) traditionally played an integral part of the Walking Race yearly income – invariably amounting to approximately between 55% and 65% of the total receipts.

Despite Steyning Breweries and the International Tea Stores withdrawing from subscribing, enough money was made in 1929 to provide for one guinea donations to Steyning Nursing Association, Sussex County Hospital, Throat and Ear Hospital and Steyning Town Band. By way of special recognition, an honorarium of four guineas was made to the Honourable Secretary, Dennis West.

List of Subscriptions, 1930.

	£	s.	d.	£	s.	d.
Mr. H. B. Bristow	1	1	0			
Mr. T. H. Fowler	1	1	0			
Mr. W. Garlick	1	1	0			
Mr. A. Littleton	1	1	0			
Capt. F. Purchas	1	1	0			
Mr. A. J. Rodda	1	1	0			
Dr. C. W. Wheeler-Bennett	1	1	0			
				7	7	0
Mr. C. B. O. Clarke	1	0	0			
				1	0	0
Mrs. A. A. Burt		10	6			
Mrs. Northey		10	6			
Mr. G. T. Breach		10	6			
Mr. A. E. Baily		10	6			
Mr. W. L. Burt		10	6			
Mr. H. W. Burt		10	6			
Dr. G. H. U. Corbett		10	6			
Brig.-Gen. G. V. Clarke		10	6			
Brig.-Gen. Grove, C.B., C.B.E.		10	6			
Messrs. G. Grigg & Sons		10	6			
Mr. L. C. Ing		10	6			
Mr. A. Linfield		10	6			
Mr. Bertram Nicholls		10	6			
Capt. H. C. Phipps		10	6			
Dr. H. H. Taylor, J.P.		10	6			
Mr. W. G. Theobald		10	6			
Mr. W. Ware		10	6			
				8	18	6
Mrs. Sapsworth		10	0			
Miss E. M. Soundy		10	0			
Rev. C. R. Attenborough, M.A.		10	0			
Mr. P. Breach		10	0			
Mr. H. T. W. Clements		10	0			
Capt. D. W. Clarke		10	0			
Mr. H. de Gruchy		10	0			
The Hon. Mrs. Howard		10	0			
Mr. E. Holmes		10	0			
The Hon. C. E. Hamilton-Russell		10	0			
Mr. G. Hodgson		10	0			
Mr. G. Hobbs		10	0			
Mr. J. How		10	0			
Mr. J. F. L. Henderson		10	0			
Mr. A. G. Marshall		10	0			
Messrs. J. K. Nye & Donne		10	0			
The late Mr. G. W. Ritchie		10	0			
Mr. F. Smart		10	0			
Mr. H. G. Sugden		10	0			
Steyning Laundry Co., Ltd.		10	0			
				10	0	0
Carried forward				27	5	6

List of subscribers, ten Shillings and over, for 1930

Compare the previous 1930 Subscriber's List to the left 1964 version. It is still a combination of individuals, local businesses, and shops with the addition of major support from sporting and leisure organisations.

List of Donations and Subscriptions—1964

	£	s	d
Mr. E. A. Adcock		5	–
Mr. E. S. Adcock		5	–
Amateur Athletics Supporters Association (Football Tickets and Draws)	55	4	2
Mr. T. F. D. Robertson Aikman		10	6
Mr. & Mrs. G. D. Baker		7	6
Mr. E. A. Ball		5	–
Mr. R. M. Ballard	1	–	
Mr. Reg. Bateman	2	2	–
Mr. R. M. Beavan	1	–	
Mr. H. E. V. Bennett	1	1	–
Mrs. E. L. Wheeler-Bennett	1	1	–
Mr. M. Blake		10	6
Mr. T. J. Bleach		10	–
Mr. C. E. Bligh		10	–
Mr. N. P. Botting		10	6
Brickwoods Ltd.	1	1	–
Mr. & Mrs. R. C. Burnett	1	–	
Mr. W. Leslie Burt 1963/4	2	2	–
Carpenter, Arnold & Turner		10	6
Mrs. S. Cassie		3	–
Mrs. J. M. Clayton	1	–	
Dr. A. Dyce Davidson	1	1	–
Mr. & Mrs. A. E. Day		10	–
Mr. A. K. Day		5	–
Mr. W. Dick		5	–
Frank Duke Limited	1	–	
Mr. P. Lorne Duncan	1	–	
Mr. J. R. A. English		10	–
Mrs. N. M. Fellowes	1	–	
Mr. F. Fennell		10	–
Mr. P. R. Blair-Fish	1	1	–
Mr. S. A. Fish	2	2	–
Mrs. H. Flowers		10	–
Miss E. M. Forbes		12	6
Mr. C. H. Franklin	1	1	–
Mr. J. B. Gibbon		10	–
Mr. C. H. Gillam		10	–
Miss H. Gluck	1	1	–
Mr. K. Green		10	–
Green Bros.		10	–
Mr. & Mrs. G. T. Greenfield		10	–
Mr. C. A. Grigg		10	6
Mr. & Mrs. Bertram Grigg		10	6
Mrs. M. Gumbrell		10	–
Mrs. W. F. Haldane		5	–
Mr. & Mrs. S. J. Harrison		15	–
Miss I. G. Hayman	1	1	–
Mr. A. E. Hazel		5	–
Miss E. S. Heald	1	1	–
Mr. J. F. L. Henderson	2	2	–
Mr. & Mrs. H. Hirst		10	–
International Stores		10	6
Mr. C. A. Jenkins	1	1	–
Mrs. C. Jesse		10	–
Mr. H. Dale Johnson		10	6

	£	s	d
The Misses J. O. Joseph	1	1	–
Mr. J. A. Lacey	2	2	–
Mr. F. W. Langridge		10	–
Adml. & Lady Little	1	1	–
Mr. W. A. Locke	1	10	–
Mr. F. J. Miller	1	–	
Mr. & Mrs. A. Frazier Mills		10	6
Mrs. D. Moss	1	1	–
Mrs. F. Naldrett		10	–
Mr. & Mrs. W. P. Neale		10	6
Mrs. C. R. E. Osmond	1	1	–
Mr. N. T. Parrott		6	6
Mr. & Mrs. F. W. Payne	1	1	–
Mr. L. A. Pelling		5	–
Mr. R. A. Penfold		10	–
Mr. A. H. G. Pope	3	–	
Mrs. M. Purchas	2	2	–
Capt. F. Purchas Memorial	5	5	–
Mr. F. B. Purchas	5	5	–
Mr. J. E. Rawlings		10	–
Mr. B. Read	1	1	–
Mr. D. C. Read		10	–
Mr. & Mrs. W. S. Read		10	6
Mr. G. H. Recknell	1	1	–
Mrs. E. M. Redfern	3	3	–
Mr. W. F. Richards		10	6
Miss S. H. Ride		5	–
Mr. A. J. Rudge		10	6
Mr. & Mrs. A. Saunders		10	–
Mrs. A. Settle	1	1	–
Mr. F. Seymour 1963/4	1	–	
Mr. & Mrs. H. W. Skinner		10	–
Mrs. L. Spillman	1	–	
Steyning Bingo Association	50	–	–
Mr. E. J. Sturt		15	–
Mr. T. Tidy	1	–	
Mr. & Mrs. D. P. Toomey	1	1	–
Mr. C. A. Treacher	1	1	–
Mr. & Mrs. Webb		4	–
Mr. & Mrs. R. P. Wells	1	–	
Wests Library		10	–
Wests Printing Works	1	1	–
Mr. A. Willows		5	–
Mr. H. L. Wills		10	–
Mr. John F. Wood		10	–
Mr. R. Woodhams		15	–
Mr. John C. Wyld		10	–
Anon		1	9
Also 21 members' subn. @ 1/– 14 @ 2/– 17 @ 3/6	5	8	6
Total of Donations and Subscriptions for year 1964	£201	5	5

34

Steyning Annual Walking Races, Balance Sheet, 1936.

RECEIPTS.	£	s.	d.	EXPENDITURE.	£	s.	d.
Balance in hand	2	8	11	Hire of Dressing Room		14	0
Entries : Seniors	1	1	0	Prizes : Seniors	20	18	0
Juniors		5	6	Juniors	6	15	0
Sale of Programmes	3	12	8	Boys	2	12	6
Donations	42	6	6	Boys' Consolations	1	4	0
Cycle Competition	6	13	10	Insurance of Cups		15	0
Profit on Dance	5	17	3	Programmes	3	7	6
Cake Competition per Mrs. Hutchings ...		16	8	Wests Printing Account	9	0	7
				S. Matthews, Medals, etc..	5	12	0
				J. Taylor, Billposting		7	6
				Postages	1	19	7
				Sundries	1	3	9
				W. Gray & Co.		6	11
				Hire of Town Hall Room		5	0
				Pianist		10	6
				A.A.A. Affiliation Fee		10	6
				St. John Ambulance	1	1	0
				Secretary's Honorarium	4	4	0
				Assistant Secretary's Honorarium	1	1	0
				Balance in hand		14	0
	£63	2	4		£63	2	4

E. HOLMES, *Hon. Treasurer.*
D. WEST, *Hon. Secretary.*

Examined with vouchers and found correct.
June 6th, 1936.   W. W. RAPLEY, *Hon. Auditor.*

Annual Accounts (Balance Sheet) from Committee Minutes Book for 1936.

Aside from Race entrance fees and programme sales in this pre World War Two period, the treasurer also received money from a cycle competition, courtesy of Frank Stubbings Cycles, which took place from 1933, the odd cake competition (Mrs. Hutchings) and watch raffle contest - the cycle competition, raised, for example, just over 10% of Race income for 1936.

STEYNING WALKING RACE.

THE NINTH ANNUAL

SMOKING CONCERT

will be held at the Headquarters,

THE

CHEQUERS HOTEL, STEYNING,

on

Thursday, May 1st,

At 7.15 p.m.,

For the Presentation of the

3 SILVER CHALLENGE CUPS,

SILVER MEDALS,

and

PRIZE VOUCHERS

to the Successful Competitors.

The Chair will be taken by

Mr. G. T. BREACH.

ALL ARE WELCOME.

A veritable combination of whist drives, dances and "Smokers" (see Glossary of Terms), additionally provided much needed income, as well as providing, on many occasions a venue for the annual prize and Race Walking Cup ceremony.

A typical example of post Race day "entertainment" on this occasion dating from 1924.

CHAPTER FIVE

THE POWER OF THE PRESS AND POLITICS

L ocal newspapers have dutifully reported the 15 mile event, originally (as far as the records show) from 1924, with a modest statement,

" *The greatest interest centred in the Steyning and District 15 miles scratch walking race yesterday* [2nd April]. *This is the ninth annual event in the series and the route was thronged in the various Adur villages through which the competition passed. The sultry weather, the condition of the roads and the heavy traffic were all against good times, and already the men were behind past performances during this contest in some other years.*"
Source: Steyning Athletic Press Cutting file – precise newspaper unknown.

Reports and articles on the 15 Mile Race, and later the Juniors' and Boys' races were faithfully published year by year, with subsequent editions in the 1920's and 1930's now referring to the "*Great Easter Monday Walking Festival*". The coverage tended to provide almost a blow by blow summary of the walkers' relative positions at various points on the course thereby portraying ongoing reporting over the entire 15 miles. Additionally as the 1931 Press Cuttings file clearly illustrates, and for that year despite the rain, "*four or five thousand people, at various places, watched the Steyning Easter Monday Walking Races*". Newspaper reports of the 1930's, up until the Second World War reflected the "*great public attraction*" of the event and with the Easter Monday Races "*popularity and success*", it was also reporting practice to refer to "*well known people in the gathering*" watching the event. For example in 1932, "*C.B.O. Clarke brought a party and others present included Mr. John and Lady Oakley, Sir William and Lady Forbes and the Conservative leader* [former and later Prime Minister] *Stanley Baldwin and his wife, with their son in law and daughter, the Hon. Arthur and Mrs. Howard,*" watched the walkers.

In 1937, a Brighton newspaper referred to "*general interest* [in the Races] *appearing greater than ever*". The article continued, "*the programme of competitors represented many very old Sussex families who had inhabited the Weald and Downland for many hundreds of years*". Press coverage continues with the 1959 editions stating that "*Steyning has lots of talent*" as 50 boys entered the Races that year.

Of some consequence was another newspaper report that led "*Steyning Athletic Club is to have a women's section*" – an aspect specifically focussed upon in a later chapter.

The 28 March 1967 edition of the Evening Argus continues to report the "*usual large crowd gathered in Steyning High Street*" on Easter Monday, "*despite the bad weather in the morning*". In the reasoned article, a total of 93 youngsters competing in the morning races reveals an increase in interest in the Races [a total of 25, 15 milers are listed in the programme that year for the afternoon race. Starting and finishing at the Chequer Inn – winner Dennis Read in 2 hours 10 minutes, 34 seconds – just one of his eleven wins – see Chapter Twelve "The Record Breakers"].

Fortunately, and quite properly newspaper reports aided by pictures now in colour, appear every year to remind us all of the unique traditions, historical significance and sportsmanlike competitive camaraderie that these Races unquestionably hold.

Note the crowd throng (1934 Race) in Steyning High Street – Chequer Inn. J. F. L. Henderson striding into view on the left to win in 2 hours 11 minutes 3 seconds.

A similar view, Steyning High Street, Chequer Inn on the right, with scaffolding, 54 years later in 1988, 15 Mile Race. Parked cars now replace, in part, the depth of the crowd – Darrell Stone romping home in record time 1 hour 47 minutes 19 seconds (see Chapter Twelve).

Separately, yet in its own particular way, local politics find a place in the annals of the Steyning Easter Monday Walking Races. In 1929, as already indicated, an amusing incident arose. It was discovered that the annual Easter Monday dance (the "Smoker") was booked in the usual hall at the same time that the local Conservatives were to have their own musical evening! Secretary West went forth to negotiate – successfully, as the Tory devotees withdrew provided the Race Walking Committee met the existing liabilities of Hall hire and orchestral fees. The Walking Race money raising dance was safe – and ticket sales progressed at 2 shillings and sixpence each. Dance profits were over £11.

Also, as mentioned, a senior political figure watched the 1931 races. Just after the 2 o'clock Fifteen Mile start, the walkers passed by Wappingthorn, just over a mile from the Steyning Town Clock, only to see the Rt. Hon. Stanley Baldwin, who was spending Easter with his daughter, Hon. Mrs. Arthur Howard – who already gave financial support to the event. Secretary and Treasurer E. Emsley dismounted from his official's bicycle to answer Baldwin's inevitable enquiries about the event. Stanley Baldwin's choice was fortunate as Emsley was a mine of information having previously taken part himself with some great spirit of interest.

The Conservative political connection was extended to the years 1932 – 1949 as Earl (later Lord) Winterton, the constituency Member of Parliament was invited to start the Senior Races. The added attraction of a luncheon provided, no doubt added flavour to his Lordship's genuine interest, equally spurred on by his appointment as a Vice President from 1934. Winterton's retention of the Horsham (North West Sussex Division, later Horsham and Worthing) Parliamentary seat was from 1904 to 1951. Originally Viscount Turnour, Winterton became an Earl on the death of his father in April 1907 but as this was an Irish Peerage, he continued to sit in the House of Commons. He was on the right wing of the Party. He was a popular choice of starter and his last recorded appearance in this role was in 1956, as the following picture reveals, and he had a great interest in the Race in his exalted capacity of a race official.

Earl Winterton with furled umbrella starting the 1932 race with Walking Race President Bertram Nicholls, on the left looking on.

CHAPTER SIX

THE JOHNNY HENDERSON INFLUENCE

Many ordinary citizens can lay legitimate claim to fame for involvement in the Easter Monday Walking Races; candidates such as Ernie Adcock, Den West, Norman Read (for his particular story, see "A Steyning Connection" by Ian Ivatt, Vernon Books, 2001), Graham Morris, Darrell Stone, et al – yet Henderson's influence, drive and special brand of the unique, mark him out for particular attention. John Florian Lennox Henderson was born, in Steyning High Street, on 27 July 1906. He had an elder brother Leonard Bertram Henderson, born on 27 August 1903. The brothers' father was John Leonard Henderson described as a solicitor's clerk in the 1903 birth records, and later on at John's birth as a lace cleaner. The boys' mother, Florence Edith, was reported as a crochet worker, schoolmistress, or magazine writer, depending upon which official document preferred. Mrs. Henderson passed on in 1925. Long term local memories recall that John was a sickly child, an aspect confirmed by Johnny himself in a 1953 newspaper article:

"*I was a weakling all right. I owe my wonderful* [subsequent] *health to walking. Every minute of it has been a pleasure, what a break for me when I entered that Steyning race in 1927.*"

After going through the educational process at Steyning, Johnny first began work as an assistant at Goachers, the Bakers, in Steyning High Street. He later went to work at Christ's Hospital School, near Horsham from 1928, where his father was also employed, to reach the position of Master of the Robes to go on to retirement in 1971.

Johnny's novice attempt at the 15 mile Easter Monday Walk was, as he says, in 1927, when he clocked up a creditable 2 hours, 41 minutes, 53 seconds, in twelfth position. In 1929 he was first home in 2 hours 22 minutes 7 seconds – to squeeze past Ernie Adcock's 1912 record by 38 seconds. He did not compete in 1930 as he had septic feet (described as "indisposed" in the Committee minutes) but returned to the fray from 1931 onwards. He was the outright winner in each of the years 1932 – 1936, and won again in 1947. A letter, from mid 1935, to Johnny from Henry Evans the retiring secretary of the Sussex County A.A.A., speaks volumes of Johnny's record at the Steyning 15 mile event. Here is an extract,

"*It was with pleasure* [that] *I got the Sussex Daily* [newspaper] *on Monday and saw you had again won incidentally breaking your own record in the Steyning Walk was another fine performance. A real Jubilee win. With best recollections of your fine sportsmanship and the very best wishes for your future*".

His 1936 best time ever of 2 hours, 9 minutes, 37 seconds, stood until Olympic Gold Medallist, Norman Read, nearly broke through the 2 hour barrier, twenty two years later in 1958. Not at all bad as Johnny was no giant and was often referred to by his contemporaries as "titch".

By now, Johnny had achieved virtual legendary status and won many Sussex (Brighton to Hastings walk, for example) and National events outside the scope of this publication. His ambition, nearly but not quite realised, was to represent his country at walking and he just missed out selection from the Berlin Olympic Games of 1936 and, had the Second World War not intervened, the proposed Helsinki Games of 1940), and again, post war in London, 1948, when he was really past his peak.

True to his beliefs and in spite of his personal disappointment, Johnny strove long and hard "*to help a youngster to bring the honour to Steyning*". This he indeed did as evidenced by his tutelage of Norman Read (see also Chapter Twelve, the Record Breakers), amongst countless others.

Johnny continued his race walking (even walking to work at Christ's Hospital) and the inevitable training – invariably starting across the South Downs when often such Sunday "strolls" went through three counties, but was called up in the Army 1940 – 1945. Even so, he managed to still race walk. The News of the World reports Johnny's participation, in 1942, in an event in North West England.

After the war, Johnny again participated in the Steyning 15 Mile events, as already mentioned, winning in 1947, and finishing in respectable positions in many years. His final appearance in the Steyning Easter Monday races was at the age of sixty two in 1969. Many walkers will well remember his enthusiasm, encouragement of youngsters, helping Juniors with Race entrance fees, programme delivery and complete professional sportsman's attitude. He was familiar throughout the County and commented himself, "*People meant to be helpful but I had to refuse dozens of lift offers and turn down invitations for meals and drinks – I was on serious [walking] business*". In the Herald, 1 September 1961, Johnny refers to his 50 mile "*strolls*" on a Sunday: "*Tom Tidy, and I like to go out training together. You couldn't keep walking at my age [55] unless you kept training regularly.*" – How true!

Johnny, moreover, deserves special mention of his later involvement as the Race Secretary, and the establishment of the club in the early 1950's. He maintained and supervised the temporary changing "facilities" for walkers in the old Air Raid shelters on the cricket pitch, at this time. He also worked to firmly establish the club premises in Charlton Street, Steyning later in 1968. In reality, no man put so many hours into the club's activities, events, sporting and social, than John Florian Lennox Henderson. He always talked to eager listeners of his hero, the great walking Race Champion, Harold Whitlock. His advice to the up and coming enthusiastic walker was "*concentrate on style, the speed will come later.*" Johnny obtained the much coveted title of "Centurion" as he walked 100 miles in less than 24 hours. Such achievers referred to one another as "Brother" in correspondence. Johnny was still actively working, and walking up in the South Downs until his death in 1981. He never married, nor smoked or drank anything strongly alcoholic.

Mrs. Fido Ashdown, specifically, has this to say: "*I shall always remember John with a smile on his face. A man of small stature but a gentleman in every sense of the word. Quite a somewhat private person, but very sociable and always pleased to stop and have a chat. I understand John lived with his mother and elder brother at Box House, opposite Betty's, in the High Street at Steyning, although John never spoke very much of his parents or family. His mother, I believe, was a very avid crochet worker. He worked at Christ's Hospital School and I remember when the pupils' pyjamas became too old to wear, he would salvage the best parts and bring them to my mother, out of which she would make dusters and sell them to her friends for sixpence, donating her 'takings' to the Methodist Church. Every Wednesday, or possibly Thursday, John would call in the evening to collect our contribution for a swindle the club used to run, and my mother would have a small bag of sweets, usually black and white bulls' eyes waiting for John. After he retired from Christ's Hospital School, his life was taken up almost entirely with the Athletic Club and he would spend hours at their Headquarters in Charlton Street. Living with my brother Ted for many years, his death was a great loss to us and even greater to the Club.*"

Christ's Hospital's own publication, "The Blue Magazine" said of Johnny, when he stood down in September 1971: "*John was appointed as 2nd assistant in the Wardrobe and was promoted to 1st assistant in 1936. He is now retiring after 43 years long and faithful service. He has measured and fitted thousands of boys during these years with new coats, breeches and shoes, and seen many changes – he will always be remembered for his unfailing good humour and courtesy to boys, masters, and staff. Nothing is ever too much trouble, and John can always be relied upon to produce any 'prop' required for School or House plays, however peculiar the request. He has a wonderful memory and the large and varied stock in the Wardrobe under his charge is meticulously kept. Such is his reputation for accuracy that, at stocktaking, if there is a slight discrepancy on any item, every available record in the office is checked before we ever think of asking Henderson to re-check his stock."*

Johnny Henderson, heading for his first win in 1929 – note, once more, the attendant cyclists.

It was in this year that Henderson temporarily moved to "Westlands", Two Mile Ash, near Horsham and thus nominally failed to meet his residential qualification to compete. However, his friend, A. E. Goacher, reserved a room for Henderson, at his Steyning house, for Johnny's use at any time – thus qualification was ensured.

Johnny Henderson (No. 4) later in 1962 – still a keen competitor. Eventual winner that year Dennis Read (no. 11), partially shielded by Ron Penfold (no. 10), who was to go on and win in 1969. Also shown Johnny Miller (no. 9) – Sussex 7 Mile Champion in 1958. The start was outside the Chequer Inn, Steyning High Street.

STEYNING AND DISTRICT ANNUAL WALKING RACES
EASTER MONDAY 1957

Promoted by Steyning Athletic Club.   Under A.A.A. Laws.

Established 1912

This is to Certify that

J. F. L. Henderson

completed the course in the

Seniors' 15 miles   Race

in 2 hours 27 minutes 9 seconds

President *J. F. L. Henderson* Hon. Secretary
STEYNING ATHLETIC CLUB.

Above: J. F. L. Henderson co-signs his own course completion certificate for the 1957 Race – in an excellent time for a 50 year old.

Right: The start of the 1973 15 Mile Race, a Champion's line-up! No. 11, R. A. Emsley (Winner 1972), No. 13, S. A. Fish (Winner 1970), No. 38 R. A. Penfold (Winner 1964, 1969), No. 43 D. J. Stevens (Winner 1973 to 1976 and winner of Stock Exchange Walking Race, at 2, 7, and 25 miles). Similarly, Centurion J. F. L. Henderson, No. 20 hidden from view by walkers, who competed first in 1927 and retired after the 1977 Race. Tom Tidy (Centurion, Veteran, No. 46) competed 1957 – 2003.

CHAPTER SEVEN

THREESOMES

There is a clear link between Steyning townspeople and the Easter Monday Walking Races – a key point running throughout this book. Entire families became involved, which could be a little expensive in subscriptions and race fees if brothers, fathers, and later mothers and daughters competed together. This section of the book looks at the commonest groupings which tended to be in threes and particularly fits into the three member "Relay Teams" which first came into being in 1988, although "team" racing with various multiple entries was permitted earlier from 1982.

As would be expected the Adcock family are represented in this chapter. The legendary Ernie, the 1912 winner, raced in the Seniors' event until 1935. His son, Trevor, who created his own separate pile of honours on the cricket field, took part in the 1951, 15 mile event. Trevor's boy, Neil, first raced as a nine year old in 1978, and again in 1979 and just for good measure, Neil's sister, Julie entered into the 1982 Girls and Ladies race.

The fabulous Boyd trio, en route in the 1952 Easter Monday Walking race. Fred Boyd, No. 8 was the Juniors' Handicap winner in 1936, Edward (Ted) Boyd, No. 7 first took part in the 1927 Boys' Race and won a one shilling prize for coming in fifth place! G. E. Boyd (Tim) entered into the Juniors' races from 1928 and the Seniors' 15 mile race in 1938 and 1939. Earliest of all, a Boyd served on the 1913 Race Walking Committee.

The Read brothers, Norman, Brian and Dennis, who especially feature in Chapter 12 "The Record Breakers", are shown here in a rare photograph, taken in Church Street, Steyning, of the 1950 Cup Winners.

Brian, third from left, Norman in the centre, behind the largest Winners Cup, and young Dennis, is second from right, in the forefront. Johnny Henderson, aged 43 years is on the extreme left.

36th ANNUAL 15-MILE RACE,

Age Limit: 16 years or over on March 20th.

ROUTE : Start at "The Chequer Inn", through Partridge Green, Henfield, Bramber and finish at "The Chequer Inn".

NOTE: *Competitors and Officials are requested to be at "The Chequer Inn" at 1.40 p.m.*

Competitors and their Numbers.

1 **C. BEAN** H (N)	15 **D. C. READ** S (Winner 1957)
2 **J. R. BETTANY** S	(Fastest Youth in
3 **B. F. EMERY** S (N)	Gt. Britain 1957)
4 **F. GATFORD** S	16 **N. R. READ** S
5 **A. B. GRIGG** S (V) (*Centurion)	(Olympic Gold Medallist
6 **J. F. L. HENDERSON** S (V)	Melbourne 1956)
(*Centurion)	17 **D. C. RIDLEY** S
(Record Time Holder 1936)	18 **R. J. RIDLEY** S (N)
7 **P. F. W. HILL** B	19 **R. H. SHEPPARD** S
8 **W. A. LOCKE** W (V) (*Centurion)	(Third Fastest Youth
9 **G. C. MAJOR** S	in Gt. Britain 1956)
10 **K. S. MAJOR** S	20 **L. W. SIBLEY** S (N)
11 **K. W. MAJOR** S	21 **T. TIDY** H
12 **P. J. W. MARCHANT** W (N)	22 **J. A. TROWER** S (Fastest
13 **F. J. MILLER** S (2nd Sussex	Youth in Gt.Britain 1956)
A.A.A. 7 miles Championship	23 **M. TROWER** S (2nd 1957)
1957)	24 **M. R. TWEED** S
14 **B. D. READ** S	25 **J. F. WOOD** W (Winner
	Intermediate Race 1957)
	26 **A. H. YARDLEY** S (V)

B=Upper Beeding.   H=Henfield.   S=Steyning.   W=Wiston.
N=Novice (one who has not won a prize for walking since reaching the age of 16 years.)
V=Veteran (over 40 years of age on March 20th.)
*A Centurion is one who has walked 100 miles within 24 hours, under A.A.A. Laws.

Starter: F. B. PURCHAS, Esq.

Judges: Messrs. R. B. COLLARD, R.W.A.,   H. A. FRY, R.W.A., A. J. SLATER, R.W.A., H. V. STAMMER, R.W.A., H. W. TYLER, R.W.A. and A. UNSTED, R.W.A.

Recorders: Messrs. M. E. MITCHELL, G. W. MUNNERY and E. A. PARROTT.

Competitors' First Aid Car: St. JOHN AMBULANCE, Steyning Section

SPECIAL NOTE.—*The Police particularly request spectators to keep on the pavements during the start and finish of each race.*

SPECIAL NOTE TO CYCLISTS

1. **Cyclists must not fall in with the Walkers until reaching Bayards.**
2. **All cyclists are requested to ride not more than two abreast and at least 10 yards behind any Walker.**
3. **In the event of a Competitor retiring, he or his attendant must report it to an Official without delay.**

Competitors must not make use of footpaths or pavements, and are particularly requested to keep to the left-hand side of the road, thus minimising the danger of accidents.

In the 1950's, the Major family of Steyning were represented in the Seniors' 15 mile walk, although their name disappears from the records after 1959.

A memorable list of the starters for the 36th Annual 15 mile race in 1958. There are three Majors, three Read Brothers, J. A. Trower, fastest youth in Great Britain 1956, and other stalwarts who are mentioned elsewhere in this book, Peter Hill, Charlie Bean (first race as a Senior), Bertram Grigg, Johnny Henderson, and W. A. (Bill) Locke, Tom Tidy, all Centurions, and last, but by no means least F. J. (Johnny) Miller. Source: Official Race Programme 1958.

Before that, in 1927, the Burr brothers, W. S., W. E. and F. E. took part together in the 1927 line-up, for the afternoon 15 mile event. W. S. Burr had the distinction of winning the first Juniors' race in 1926.

The official photograph of the 15 mile Race entrants and officials in 1927. The Burr brothers are numbered 13 (W.S.B.), 21 (W.E.B.), and 22 (F.E.B.) – holder of the Novices and Handicap cups. Chairman of Race Committee, G. T. Breach, as a novice walker, No. 6. As indicated in Chapter 2, W. E. Burr was subject to a residential enquiry, after the 1929 race, on the claim, in the Minute Book, that his house was "thought to be just outside of Steyning Parish and that this fact might debar him". The wise head of Committee member, and local artist, Bertram Nicholls saved the day by persuading the committee unanimously to regard Burr as "in the strict meaning is a Steyning man".

The Nunn boys of Upper Beeding significantly dominated the Boys' and Junior races in the 1980's. Richard Nunn first raced as an 8 year old in 1980, and he went on to win the Boys' race in 1982, 1983, the Juniors' race in 1985, and the Intermediate Men's Races in 1988 and 1989 – later an International. His older brother Paul also swiftly reached Junior International level in 1985 – 1986 to then progress to the 15 mile event in 1987. Meanwhile young Jamie Nunn appears in the 1986 programme competing as a 10 year old, to go on to win the next year as an eleven year old in a course record time (10 minutes 14 seconds). He won again as a Junior in 1988 to smash yet another course record at 28 minutes 30 seconds, whilst his older brother, Richard, that same year achieved another course record in the Intermediate section at 26 minutes 21 seconds. In 1989 and 1990, he also won the Junior Men's races.

During this time, their father, Ian Nunn managed the quite separate role of Course Marshall and Judge. He was also responsible for the school and annual schools report in the Race Programme. It was of course calculated that encouragement of school children could lead to later club membership and he was also mentor and advisor to the boys, and even managed to compete in the 15 mile event himself!

Richard Nunn 1988

Paul Nunn 1988

Jamie Nunn 1989

The Stratford family of Steyning also took part in the Boys and Juniors races in the 1950's. The 1956 official Race Programme lists the nine year old C. G. Stratford taking part, with A. J. Stratford, who went on to be a Junior racer, "C. G." appears again in the 1957 and 1958 programmes. Brother T. J. joins in 1958, the 27th annual Boys' Race, so that all three take part that year. None of them won!

There are also the three Ford-Dunn girls; Liz, Sue, and Helen. They have all walked the 15 Mile Easter Monday event, both the full distance each and, moreover, as part of relay teams. Helen went on to achieve national champion status, whilst Liz and Sue have been County champions. All three sisters were in the Steyning Athletic Club Ladies Team that represented Great Britain in Italy in 2001.

The last threesome included in this chapter is the Bean family of Henfield, although Charlie Bean has his own special mention in "The Record Breakers – Chapter Twelve". Sons John, Richard, and daughter Mary Bean also appear together for the first time in the 1978 Race Souvenir Programme (price 10 pence), to be joined by Carol Bean (Charlie's now former wife) for the first year of the Ladies Races in 1980.

Threesomes tend to increase as other kith and kin begin to race. For a further study of this phenomenon, other family groups – in increased numbers – are included in Chapter Twelve.

The front page of the official Race Day programme. This was the final year that use was made of the 1923 logo of two Edwardian walkers.

SOUVENIR PROGRAMME 25p

STEYNING & DISTRICT
Annual
Walking Races

Open to Steyning, Wiston, Ashurst, Bramber, Beeding, Small Dole, Dacre Gardens, Henfield, Shermanbury and Partridge Green.

on EASTER MONDAY, 20th APRIL, 1987

Established 1912.

Promoted by the Steyning Athletic Club
(Under A.A.A. Laws)

Hon. Race Secretary & Club Hon. Secretary:
Mr. D. J. STEVENS
23 Roman Road, Steyning   Telephone: 814422

Sponsored by

J. THOMAS (SOUTHERN) LTD.

WITH COMPLIMENTS

CHAPTER EIGHT

BOOTS AND CLOTHING

During the 100 years that this book covers, there has been a huge change in the Race Walking apparel. As pointed out in the earlier picture of the first Easter Monday Race walkers of 1903, the type of boots worn covered not just the foot but also the ankle area, even a little beyond in some instances.

Equally, as will be swiftly detected from those Race photographs included in this work, boot types of footwear, not necessarily the standard black colour, were used by competitors. Boys and Juniors tended to wear, no doubt in many cases, for economic reasons during the 1920's and 1930's a wide variety of footwear including the inevitable canvas shoe.

Almost without exception, in the early days, white socks were worn by the Senior Racers and the 1912 picture of George (Carrots) Holden as depicted in Chapter Twelve provides an excellent example of both typical ankle socks of the time and the style of boot he favoured.

By the onset of the 1950's, footwear became more standardised and the "Whitlock" boot, named after the great Olympic Champion of 1936, Harold Whitlock, became the much desired shoe or boot. The Whitlock footwear also had a further advantage to the Race Walking devotee who rapidly wore out his boots. This famous boot had, in addition to leather uppers and a covering tongue and laces (effectively to keep out stones from getting into the boot during a race), a rubber sole that could be simply stripped off and replaced. These "Whitlock" favourites were worn by some Racers with the sock having an elasticated piece going under the boot to keep the sock, hopefully, in place – and, once again, to exclude flints and small stones from entering.

In modern times, the keen Club Walker, who takes part in Walking Races throughout the year would prefer the trainer type equivalent, or even, for those at the top of Walking Race ability, the coveted personalised race shoe.

Robert Rice, already featuring in Chapter 3, summarises his own thoughts on race walking apparel, used after the Second World War: -

"In the morning races, competitors wore vests, shorts, and plimsolls. As the 50's progressed, the shorts got shorter presumably following the fashion of footballers. Compare pictures of Stanley Matthews and Bobby Moore, the former with knee length shorts, the latter with naked thighs. The 15 mile was quite different. The real sporty types, Norman Read, Olympic gold medallist et al wore the proper vest, shorts and plimsolls; the majority of men wore sometimes vests or ordinary shirts, shorts and more often than not, ordinary shoes and calf-length socks. These were the really good 'sports' that walked the 15 miles just for fun."

As far as other race clothing is concerned, the club colours after the 1950's, were a white vest, singlet or shirt (later with a black stripe) and dark or black shorts – at least officially. With the advent of tracksuits, shorts – at least after 1970 – began to change shape and walkers, especially the youngsters now turned out in a variety of styles and colours – thus mirror imaging the distinct changes of sportswear in other sporting events, such as tennis, cricket, or athletics. For the boys the shorts now preferred were white, red or blue – even all of these – including the new wonder fabric Lycra, and the Senior 15 milers, whilst adapting to this change, were more conservative in their choice of colours, sweatshirts and vests. Ladies racing now turned out in even more interesting styles and colours. Tight "knickers" were worn, as were looser shorts, in contrasting manner (1989 Ladies Race).

THE THREE STAGES OF FOOTWEAR:

The start of the 1929 Seniors' 15 mile race with an assortment of footwear.

The 1955 Seniors' race; note the standardised black socks and black boots, the legs of No. 24, R. Sibley, on the left and No. 13, A. B. Grigg, on the right.

The 1989 15 Mile Race start – note the preponderance of trainer type shoe, even custom made footwear, in some instances.

Jill Trower

Jean Bleach

DIFFERING FASHIONS AND STYLES IN 1990

Seniors' 15 Mile Race – predominantly men

Senior Ladies, Junior Ladies, and Novice Ladies

The start of the 2003 15 Mile Race including Ladies – showing a full variety of loose and tight fitting shorts, tracksuits, and colours – author Ian Ivatt, No. 171 on the far right, seemingly taking an early, yet totally temporary lead, only for 100 yards.

Source: West Sussex County Times, Friday, 25 April 2003.

CHAPTER NINE

AMATEUR ATHLETIC ASSOCIATION ~ A CLUB IS FORMED

As already described, in the very early days of Race Walking the entire responsibility for organising these Easter Monday Races fell upon the "Race Walking Committee". The question of an "official" identity for the race was raised as far back as 1922 when one plucky committee member proposed some "overseeing" by the Amateur Athletic Association (A.A.A.). In 1923, the committee voted upon whether any affiliation with this sports body was preferred, only to dismiss such an idea. There the matter rested for ten years, although in the 1929 Races "A.A.A." scouts were asked to watch the event – positioning themselves at "dangerous corners".

In 1933, the Association took the initiative and suggested that the Steyning Easter Monday Walking Races become registered under the A.A.A. laws. This time feelings had changed and the A.A.A. were invited to send representatives for advice and discussions. The group deputation obligingly arrived and made an official presentation of their case. The end result of this was for the Committee to vote upon the issue – to produce a reverse of the 1923 verdict by opting for future affiliation (34 votes for, none against).

The immediate effect of this was to invite official Judges for the course from 1934 – with a formal request to lunch before the race, with an official "handicapper" – a situation that occurred for several consecutive years. Indeed the 1935 newspaper reports depict the Steyning 15 mile event as "a highly popular race in the A.A.A. calendar". The Race Walking Committee sent a letter of appreciation to the Association, after the races.

In the years immediately preceding the Second World War, a sub-committee was established to have another look at the race (one result of which was to allow walkers resident in Partridge Green and Henfield to now compete) and decided to submit their findings in 1938 to the A.A.A. for consideration and formal approval.

Effectively, walk racing, apart from some Juniors' and Boys' events in 1940, including evacuees (see Chapter 11) came to a halt during the Second World War, to restart in 1946. Maurice Chatfield winner both immediately before the War in 1939 was clearly still very able as he went on to achieve a win in 1946.

Nevertheless, wartime pressures and post war social changes were reflected in a desire for a proper club status. Simply using former air raid shelters situated in the cricket field for changing rooms was no longer good enough. The compromises and acceptances of "mucking in" were challenged in the new expectations of the 1950's.

Forming a much desired club, with all the implications and benefits was one thing, organising decent premises was another. However, club status was clearly desirable and the "club" was formally established in that same Festival year. The notification from President Wilfred How, himself a seasoned 15 mile campaigner, dated February 1951 confirms that the Steyning Athletic Club was officially formed, to replace the former "Sports Meeting Committee". Furthermore, the former promoters of the Steyning and District Annual Walking Races would transfer its functions with all assets and liabilities to the new club. The Easter Monday event proceeded under A.A.A. laws and the annual programme carried this front or second page endorsement from that time until the size and format of the programme altered in 1992.

The A.A.A. Race permit fee in 1950, for example, was 1 guinea, and from the moment of inception in early 1951, the club became affiliated to the Amateur Athletic Association – to effectively answer the question first proposed in 1923. Had a registered affiliated Club been available earlier then top class Steyning walkers, such as Johnny Henderson, would not have needed to join the nearest "proper" club at Brighton to achieve personal accreditation. Indeed numerous honours would have been in the name of the Steyning Club. Fortunately, this aspect was, accordingly no longer a problem, yet the earnest quest for premises now took on a new meaning.

Fortunately, a former President, Lewis Wood (1906 – 2002) provided a response by donating a piece of land, in Steyning's Charlton Street, consisting of old garages, to the club. The Club's Headquarters Appeal brochure earlier in November 1962 sets out the following financial objectives.

"Personal Donations in the region of £1,500 have been promised, and the Club, by its own efforts over the past eleven years, has built up a Headquarters Reserve Fund of £600.

The National Playing Fields Association, under the Presidency of H.R.H. The Duke of Edinburgh, has recognised the importance of this Appeal and the desirability of the provision of the facilities referred to below and has agreed to make a Grant of £300 together with a Loan of £400 repayable over 10 years."

The Special General Meeting notification of 25 January 1951 to discuss forming an Athletic Club with full affiliation to the A.A.A.

STEYNING & DISTRICT
WALKING RACES
Under A.A.A. Laws.

A Special General Meeting

TO FORM AN ATHLETIC CLUB TO BE AFFILIATED TO THE A.A.A.

will be held at the

JANE PENFOLD INSTITUTE

CHURCH STREET, STEYNING, on

Thursday, 25th January, 1951
at 6.45 p.m.

Chairman :
BRIGADIER W. R. F. OSMOND, C.B.E.

Supporters and all interested are cordially invited to attend.

J. F. L. HENDERSON, Hon. Sec.

Wests Printing Works, Steyning

Negotiations between the donor's legal advisers and the Club's solicitors proceeded later throughout 1965 allied to strenuous fund raising endeavours by the Club. Grant sources were trawled and interest free loan funds remorselessly tapped – all to add to the club's own available cash.

Outline planning permission was quickly obtained. The days of changing in converted wartime air raid shelters, having no windows, water or sanitation, were now clearly numbered. A new Headquarters, with up to date facilities included for training, coaching, changing rooms for both members and visiting clubs, plus a Club Secretary's office – all on one storey (but with an option for two) – it was now more than a dream.

After building and final inspection, the club premises were declared ready for use.

STEYNING ATHLETIC CLUB

THE OFFICERS AND COMMITTEE
have pleasure in inviting you to attend
THE OFFICIAL OPENING
of the
NEW HEADQUARTERS
at CHARLTON STREET, STEYNING, by
THE PRESIDENT: Mrs. M. PURCHAS
on THURSDAY, 18th APRIL, 1968, at 7.30 p.m.

The official invitation.

Below are selected extracts from Club Secretary Dave Steven's letter to the Sports Council of 14 February 1978 in connection with a grant application to assist funding for the second and final storey to the Club premises in Charlton Street, Steyning.

His Valentine's Day appeal was successful! The detail shown also embraces the modern day Treasurer's ideals as set out in Chapter Four.

"We have started a 200 Club recently, which has begun well as we have nearly 100 members already.

We will now be making an appeal to our supporters and benefactors who have been so wonderful to us in the past. In the appeal, I will be mentioning that the offer of interest free loans would be a great help to us and we already have a substantial amount promised to us in this way.

The Club's bank have been contacted regarding a loan and are very sympathetically inclined to us.

You will probably have seen statements of the club's year and accounts in your files, but I enclose copies of the last few years' figures in case you have not. These will show that the club has a good record of fund raising.

a) *Our Headquarters have always been much sought after by people and organisations wishing to hire the hall, and in the last few years, with the taxman taking his cut of our rather low charges, we have tended to let, in the main, only to two or three organisations who use the hall every week. Now we will not be subject to Corporation Tax and the hiring of the hall would be more beneficial. Together with more realistic charges this would prove to be, I am sure, a very real contribution.*

b) *We have an expanding membership as befits a successful club, and although our subscriptions, by athletic club standards, are low, members have always been encouraged to help on the fund raising side, which is usually evident at our Garden Fetes, Christmas Fayres, Jumble Sales, etc. I feel certain that our members' extra efforts will be shown in the coming year.*

From our headed notepaper you will see that, although the Club was not founded 'till 1951, our roots are much older, going back to 1912. Our Easter Monday races are a tradition in Steyning, which grew bigger over the years to such an extent that our club was formed to foster athletics, but especially walking, in the area. I mention these facts really to assure you that there is very little likelihood of the club foundering, because tradition always dies hard and the whole town is behind us, we could not have raised the money we have without them."

Secretary (and top race walker himself) Stevens' Appeal later touches on the main underlying theme of this book; the tradition factor and the point that the Easter Monday Walking Races have the support of the entire town.

Dave Stevens' background was in stockbroking in the City and it appears he then aspired to be a tax expert!

The reproduced photograph of the Club Headquarters in Charlton Street, Steyning, now ten years later, with the second storey added to the building, in 1978.

EASTER MONDAY WALKING RACES — THANKS

———

The Committee wish to express their sincere thanks to all who contribute in so many different ways to the success of these old established races, including:

THE POLICE — For keeping the traffic and race walkers moving freely together.

ST. JOHN AMBULANCE — Always close at hand with help and a sympathetic word.

THE LADIES — Among many other things, supplying refreshments in the Club House and helping in timekeeping and recording.

TANNOY — John Lees and Reg Wells, their first class knowledge of the sport make interesting listening.

JUDGES — Phil Collins (Chief Judge) who is assisted by many R.W.A. Judges, travelling from as far away as the Midlands.

TIMEKEEPERS AND RECORDERS — Rex Morris (Chief) and his assistants: How do they cope in the morning?

To all those not mentioned, for giving up their holiday time to to make an enjoyable day for hundreds of others.

———

TO ALL PROSPECTIVE WALKERS FOR NEXT YEAR
REMEMBER THESE DATES

EASTER MONDAY: 20th APRIL 1987
ENTRIES CLOSE: 30th MARCH 1987

A typical acknowledgement and thanks as contained in the 1986 "Souvenir Programme" priced 25 pence.

CHAPTER TEN

AT LAST - LADY WALKERS

The matter of female participation in the race walks is not new. As far back as 1923, no doubt in the wake of the enlightened new found equality status of women in the post war era, one committee member proposed that "a Girls' Walking Race be held". The other committee members unanimously disagreed, and the race walking minutes were noted: - *"That this committee gives no support to any other event held on the same day as the 'Race'."*

At the Annual General Meeting following in January 1932, the issue was raised again. On this occasion, there were four votes in favour of the motion (of admitting women to racing) and four against. It was only the casting vote of Chairman Breach that retained the status quo – and it remained thus for the next half century. Perhaps it was no coincidence that immediately after the vote the then President of the Race Walking Committee, Dr. Wheeler-Bennett promptly resigned on the basis that he would make way for those with fresh ideas.

However, by 1959 efforts were again made for female involvement. On this occasion, when the Club's first ever lady President was in office (Hon. Mrs. M. Hamilton-Russell) a clear decision was made to establish a "Women's Section" under the leadership of Jill Bettany until a committee could be formed.

As it was, female competitive race walking arrived in 1977 in the shape of the "Girls' Race" of one mile 552 yards length. This new event started at the usual Steyning Town Clock, went on to Goring Road, Cripps Lane, Church Street, and then back to the Town Clock. Was it of some coincidence that this same year there was a third Lady President of the club, Mrs. Marjorie Dingemans?

As the year 1980 dawned, a new spirit emerged. The first annual Ladies Walk, a scratch race (over 16 years of age and older on 20 March 1980) took place. Officials were appointed to oversee the competition and the late Lewis Wood, Past President of the Club offered a new Rose Bowl to the lady achieving the fastest time. The first three ladies home (the route was the same as the 1977 Girls' Walk) received trophies and consolation prizes, plus certificates were presented to all those that completed the course. Those who took part were Mesdames Bean, Donkin, Flowers, Kennard, Lesage, Page, Rose, Stevens, Watt, and Wythe. It was a milestone yet official inclusion in the 15 mile race still eluded the fair sex – until 1992 with a minimum age of 18 for both men and women.

Sarah Sowerby, previously Sarah Brown, tells her story.
"My brother Gareth took part in the Easter Monday Races as a seven year old in 1976. I used to cycle beside him as he trained around the 'Goring Road' course. In the summer of that year, there were some one mile races in the cricket field. I took part, did quite well and joined the Athletic Club and started racing for them in September 1976. At that time there were of course no Easter Monday Walking Races at all for girls and ladies.

I took part in the first Easter Monday Girls' Race in 1977 around the Goring Road course. In 1978, the first floor of the Athletics Club was being built so we had to change at the nearby S.M.E. factory.

In 1979, I got left behind at the start, still trying to get my tracksuit off and everyone else was off down the high street. The adrenalin flowed and I managed to catch everyone up except Helen Ringshaw, my biggest rival, who beat me by only 12 seconds.

Whether I would have beaten her starting at the same time I will never know – I missed out on three wins in a row anyway. When I reached 18 years of age, we raced down to Upper Beeding and back in the Ladies Race. Later this course was switched to the one kilometre lap that is now used as it appeared to be more spectator friendly. This meant that we had to race five laps of that course. This was subsequently condensed to three laps, which helped reduce the time taken to get through the other [Easter Monday] morning events more quickly, as well as endeavouring to encourage more novices to take part. Obviously this meant the event was less of a contest for me and I was happy to accept the challenge of the 15 mile race when it came to an official event for women.

I first competed in the Easter 15 mile race in 1994. One of my close rivals, Joanne Pope had won it the previous year having competed in the morning race beforehand. Unfortunately, I felt obliged to race in both (18 miles!) so our times were comparable! I finished in a time of 2 hours 21 minutes and 11 seconds. This was a new record. This was a silver standard (before women were given different standard times). In 1995, I decided to concentrate on the 15 mile race, and was really pleased to better my time by nearly 2 minutes, finishing in 2 hours, 19 minutes and 17 seconds. This was a men's gold standard and is still the course record for ladies today."

Leslie Ashby, after joining the ladies section of the Steyning Athletic Club, tells her own story of involvement in Race Walking. Her narrative is all the more remarkable as Lesley, with her two companions Jeannie Bleach and Jo Hesketh, entered the 15 mile event in 1989 without official blessing, yet received a tumultuous welcome from spectators and fellow walkers alike.

"Easter Monday 1988 was looming and for the first time, there was a novice ladies 3 kilometre race. I qualified for this, as I had not entered any races as a Steyning walker. I got very keen and would go out training on my own, when the children were at school. As I usually did the same route, I got to know a lot of people and received a lot of encouragement. Easter Monday dawned and I was so very nervous but I came first much to my family's delight and mine.

By Easter Monday 1989, I felt part of the ladies section and although I was the slowest, I didn't get totally left behind. Liz Ford Dunn and Jo Hesketh had graduated to the ladies section by now and we all got on very well. Charlie Bean and Ian Nunn helped with our training a lot and were very supportive.

Lesley, Jo, and Jeannie in the 15 mile event of 1991.

Jo Hesketh and I decided that we would like to enter the London Marathon and so on Sunday mornings we would go out and attempt longer distances. We had built up to about 13 miles when we heard that we had been rejected. After all the hard training we were obviously very disappointed and so we thought we would try to persuade those organising the Easter Monday 15 Mile to let ladies enter. Martin Hesketh totally supported us, but to no avail. Jean then suggested that the three of us enter the race unofficially. Apparently, Carol had done it previously. So, in 1990, Jo, Jean, and myself, wearing matching bright yellow vests with SAC Ladies on the front and our names on the back, took part in the 15 mile. We stuck together and finished in a time of about 2 hours 45 minutes. We received an enormous amount of support and encouragement and it was great fun in spite of a sleet storm at Small Dole and Jo almost suffering from hypothermia – but she would not give in. We were making a statement that ladies could do this walk and she kept going. With a lot of encouragement from Jean when we were climbing Clays Hill, we made it. It was a shame we didn't get a medal because that was the only time I did it."

Lesley later went on to the London Marathon in 1991, but no longer undertakes race walking owing to a back injury.

Ladies Racing and walking styles 1991. Sarah Brown 41, Philippa Savage (Junior) 64, Joanne Pope 44, Gill Trower, partly obscured 45. The Senior Ladies' race was first held in 1980. This has been walked over several different courses. For 1988, five laps of the town circuit was used to produce a distance of 5 kilometres, reduced to three laps in 1994, and now renamed "Over Elevens" Race, as merged with Junior and Intermediate Ladies.

CHAPTER ELEVEN

CHARACTERS, MYTHS AND TRADITIONS

Over the entire period of study, almost with certain regularity, numerous tales, often embellished and with many a myth has been born. Additionally, there have always been the attendant traditions connecting ordinary townsfolk with the Easter Monday Walking Races.

In the first race in 1903, there are reports that walkers who failed to complete the 15 Mile course were collected (where they fell!) by the Steyning coal cart – true or false? Chris Tod of Steyning Museum believes it is true.

Take George "Carrots" Holden as another example. Undoubtedly his nickname belied his auburn hair, yet the 1997 Race Programme claims

"For a number of years, George 'Carrots' Holden, a coalman, would work all morning on Easter Monday, bagging coal at 'Holmes' the local coal merchant. When the clock chimed 1.30 p.m., he would put down his shovel, and walk to the Steyning Tea Gardens, where he tucked into the largest steak they had. He then lined up for the start of the race at 2.00 p.m. and would walk around the course in his hob nail boots, bent forward from the waist up due to his work."

Could all that be true?

Then again, did W. A. (Bill) Locke, wearing his

The ever cheerful Bill Locke, who last raced the 15 mile event in 1959.

famous beret with the never ceasing grin, really collect primroses around the 15 mile circuit, only to hand these to some lucky spectator at the finish line? Apparently so, or was this a myth?

Again, from the 1997 Programme: *"Tim Bean watched his 18 year old son Charlie, (now one of the club's renowned coaches) walk through Henfield High Street in his first 15 mile race. After running to Henfield Railway Station, Tim Bean was able to catch a train to Steyning where he arrived in the High Street just in time to see Charlie cross the line to win the Novice's Cup in a record 2 hours, 30 minutes and 31 seconds."*

Earlier still, when Charlie was a young lad, living at Shipley in the immediate years after the Second World War, it is strongly rumoured that, on occasions Charlie took short cuts across the edge of Hilaire Belloc's (writer, poet and diarist) garden at Shipley Mill – only to raise the elderly man's anger. Apparently, Belloc bellowed at Charlie's impudence – Belloc had enough practice at that as he shouted from time to time as a Liberal M.P. for Salford South in the Liberal Governments of 1906 – 1910.

There is also a country and western song entitled "Charlie's Shoes" by Billy Walker – although one suspects there is little connection here with race walking!

Sarah Sowerby has indicated that her grandmother, who is now aged 93 and has lived in Steyning all her life, tells stories of when her brothers used to race walk and a few competitors used to get lifts on bicycles some of the way!

Are these tales fact or fiction? Let us hope that at least some of them are true!

During both World Wars, Race Walking was temporarily suspended – yet was it totally? Not quite so, it would seem, as there was still the 14th Annual Boys' Race held in 1940, with the inclusion of evacuees who were still in Steyning.

The 1940 Boys' Race competitors, 41 in number of which 10 have been identified as evacuee children.

Neil Sorrell, brother of Martin (Chapter Three) puts forward his own characterisation of the Easter Monday Walking Races in the early 1950's when he competed as a youngster – as he emphasises – just the once! Neil's story includes a mention of his own feelings, laced with some innocent boyish cynicism, yet is clearly proud to take part and have a race number pinned on his white shirt.

"As for me, I did not do much! I seem to remember a mixture of peer-pressure and allied feeling that it was something one had to do at least once, so I did take part just the once. I vaguely remember they had all sorts of groups – I think there was a Boys', Juniors', Intermediate, etc. and I'd be pretty sure I entered in the very bottom group (presumably Boys'). I think the most thrilling bit, other than being obviously on show, was getting to wear that number on my shirt. I remember wearing all white, as I think it was the expected gear. I vaguely remember pounding along Goring Road, chatting to my friends. I came in nowhere of course, but I think everyone got some kind of prize (which may have been the real incentive for taking part!) and I seem to remember mine (and probably just about everyone else's) was a penknife (of all things!). The ceremony was hardly anything: something like turning up later at St. Andrew's Hall or similar dingy village hall and collecting the item as if it were so much lost property.

Probably the most enduring memory for a small boy was all those hairy, wiry legs and grunts as the real men came in along the High Street after what I thought to be a walk around the whole of West Sussex – and of course the funny way they moved their arms and minced along."

Interestingly enough, a Steyning Church of England clergyman took part in the Easter Monday races for a number of years in the late 1980's and early 1990's. The Revd. Canon Peter Burch (whose first career was in accountancy) now gives his views on the race, making the link between the race itself, supporters, and spectators.

"My memory is that I took part in all the nine races that took place when I was Vicar [in Steyning] *from 1986 to 1994 – I have plaques for all years apart from 1991 and 1992, which are missing. The first two years I was outside the three hour set limitation but on the other seven occasions, just under it. The only other Clergyman who took part, who I only vaguely heard about, was Free Church and possibly was disqualified for some reason in the past. I did a modest amount of training – about only once a week, for up to two months* [before the race] *with Bill Proctor. I wore my South London Harriers vest in the races – I ran with them from 1953 to 1960 and have subsequently been a non-active member for 43 years. I have managed to keep pretty fit over the years so enjoyed the Steyning races. It was quite a challenge to get home in under three hours. The events were well organised, there was a friendly spirit amongst the walkers and there was good support from the crowds in a number of places*

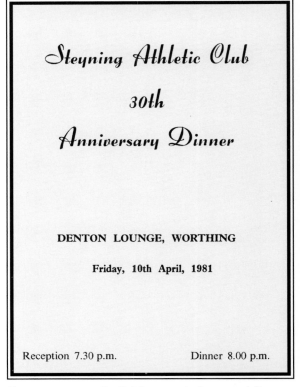

Steyning Athletic Club

30th

Anniversary Dinner

DENTON LOUNGE, WORTHING

Friday, 10th April, 1981

Reception 7.30 p.m.   Dinner 8.00 p.m.

For some years now the Club has organised an annual dinner function. Walkers still need to eat!

around the course. I certainly knew I had been in a 15 mile walking race when I finished each time, but I only really suffered on my first race when I had leg muscle cramp – yet I still managed to finish. As the Vicar, I thought the races were most appropriate on Easter Monday as they resembled the walk to Emmaus and back to Jerusalem on the first Easter Day (Luke 24, v. 13 – 35) – seven miles each way, i.e. 14 miles in all. The first year I entered, we also had a team from St. Andrew's Church called the 'Clompers'!"

Rumour has it that Peter even competed in ecclesiastical coloured purple racing shorts – true or false?

As has been seen, the Easter Monday Walking Races, which now are not just a tradition but also hold that special fascination for walkers, helpers, and spectators alike. Very few, only the well trained, much practised and expert walkers achieve the coveted accolade (and cup) as a winner. All participants, it pleasingly seems, believe that the taking part is the most relevant aspect and here, one such regular and respected 15 miler, relates his own story.

Martin Coleman has the following recollections: *"My initial memories of Easter Monday were from my late father, Reg. He told me about Norman Read, leaving this country and emigrating to New Zealand to race walk for them as he was finding the Great Britain team selection difficult, a story line then like 'Chariots of Fire'.*

My first training for the Easter Monday Walks was given to me by one of my neighbours (I think his name was Jeffery Erbs) around Coombe Road, in Steyning, where I then lived, now known as a favourite training course for sprints. On Easter Sunday of my first Easter Monday walk in 1963, my father took me for our usual family amble around the 'Lower Horseshoe' downs path. There he spotted a pigeon's nest, climbed up the tree and produced two eggs (it was legal then). He said I could have them for my breakfast the next day, and I would 'fly' around the course – that I did, unfortunately I flew over my own feet outside Kevin Golds' house by the telephone box at the bottom of Station Road, and cut my knee, not enough to stop me finishing a reasonably 12th, however. In those days, we walked from the clock tower to Goring Road, back along to Church Street, finishing at the clock tower. All of us boys (no girls then) changed into our kit, in what is now West's printing works, which was C. F. Wood and Sons' car showroom, loaned to the club by the late Lewis Wood. Coincidentally, when I was sixteen, I went to work for C. F. Wood and Son.

I competed in three Boys' Easter Monday races but then dropped out at age eleven, as the race was to Upper Beeding and back – it seemed endless miles to a young lad – yet feels like you are nearly home when competing in the 15 mile race!

Recollections of the 15 mile race are centred around my uncles from the Collyer family, some finishing, some retiring with blisters, supporting them with drinks, whilst cycling the course for the 50th Anniversary. The first memories of the 15 mile races and winners, as a lad growing up in the 1960's were of watching the finish to see who was going to be first past the tape. Would it be Dennis Read or Ron Penfold, with Johnny Henderson not far behind – these battles seemed to go on year after year until a new walker moved into Breach Close, where I was then living – Dave Stevens. Dave was to dominate the Easter Monday walks for four years. I next remember Graham Morris taking over – he was the first to break the two hour barrier [see Chapter Twelve – The Record Breakers], Norman Read having previously held the record of 2 hours and 1 second, on his first Easter Monday Race after winning his Gold Medal, about three years later. I have heard it said, that there were so many cars and people watching Norman around the entire course that day, it slowed him down enough to miss the magical beating of the two hour barrier. Finally, on to the record holder for wins – Darrell Stone [also see Chapter 12],

I would normally be in Henfield when Darrell would be finishing – some 6 miles behind. [Although the author would probably still be looking for Partridge Green and casting anxious glances behind should George Cockman catch him up.] That is the spirit of Easter Monday, not only is winning the initial objective, it is also the importance of taking part that really counts.

My first 15 mile was hindered by badly twisting my ankle the week before the race but not to be put off, I took part, yet failed to beat the 3 hour limit, not due to my ankle but by an unhelpful policeman who was supervising the temporary traffic lights at Bines Bridge, and stopped me walking through the red light owing to the repairs then being carried out - how I pleaded with him to let me go through – no chance!

Later, I finally broke the 3 hour barrier – thanks to Charlie Bean's training sessions – what fun they have been – for all of us that have been fortunate to take part and this also goes for my wife and my four children. Last year it was rumoured the race may be the last 15 mile event – so far unfounded. 100 years of history should not just be swept under irksome regulations and official 'red tape'."

Martin Ford-Dunn, an experienced walker, who first featured in the 15 Mile event from 1983 provides, below, an excellent account of his involvement in the race as a member of a relay team. This concept became increasingly popular over the years and is, in many eyes, now one of the established traditions of Easter Monday.

"In the late 1980's there was a drive to increase the number of competitors who took part in the races, and after much discussion, it was agreed that I should look at the possibility of creating a relay race for novice teams. The existing novice race was for teams of three, the aggregate time for the three walkers over the 15 miles determining the winning team. It was decided that the course be split into three legs, up to Partridge Green, Partridge Green to Henfield, and Henfield to Steyning. The changeover points would be situated at the pubs in the towns, with the expressed intention of getting Pub Teams to compete. These gave distances of 5.5, 3.5 and 6 miles, and it was thought that these would be ideal distances for any team of reasonably fit men to take on. We circulated information and entry forms to every business, shop, and organisation in the area, and delivered entry forms to every house in Partridge Green, Henfield, and the adjacent villages. I organised three teams from Ricardo Consulting Engineers, of people who met the entry criteria for living in the area, and a number of other groups provided a further five teams. Naturally, as I had convinced my fellow workmates that the race was an achievable happening, I had to take part. I took the first leg, and by the time I got to Ashurst, my shins felt red hot and were solid. The pain gradually wore off, and I made it to the changeover point in just about 1 hour and 5 minutes. I decided to continue walking so as to free off the legs. It seemed to get a lot easier, and I even began to catch up the man I had handed over to. At the halfway point, at the Bull, I was given my time as 1 hour and 29 minutes, and decided to see if I could compete the full distance. I received great encouragement through Beeding, Bramber and up the wicked Clays Hill, approaching Steyning and finally reached the finish line in about 3 hours 5 minutes. As I had only entered the Relay race, I was not given an official time, but I had proved to myself that I could get round, and that with a little more training I would be able to beat the magic 3 hour time. The next year, we changed the rules to allow the lead walker in the relay team to do the full race if he so desired. That year, I put in more training, as I was helping out with the training of the younger age groups, and I thought that I was getting reasonably fast. I entered as part of a team and also entered for the full distance. The race was a bit of a disaster. I tried to stay with some of the club's actual race walkers and by the hill at Ashurst, my shins were worse than the previous year, and I did not think I could make it to Partridge Green. However, with my team yelling me on, I got to the changeover point in around an hour. I continued, as best I could, but had to drop out at Small Dole, as I was no longer in control of the direction

I wanted my legs to go. I was determined that the following year I would not be part of a relay team, but would concentrate on doing the full distance [which indeed Martin went on to do].

Martin now concludes his contribution with a valid summary

"All along the organising committee have had to balance the traditions of the event with a need to maintain its existence in the face of all the distractions and complications of life today, which are so different to those of 1903. This competition was an event for the men of Steyning" [although later open to women, as shown in the previous chapter].

CHAPTER TWELVE

THE RECORD BREAKERS

In the final chapter, a focus upon record breaking achievements and walkers is undertaken, although not totally in connection with winning times in the Easter Bank Holiday Races.

As has already been seen in the earlier chapter "Threesomes", the tendency was for local family groups to invariably become involved in the races; yet, some families seem to be repeatedly cropping up over the years. The Bean family has five mentions, as do the Ford-Dunn's, Gretton's six, and best of all different members of the Fish family of Small Dole feature at least eight times since 1959, throughout the 1960's, with (previously an outstanding junior record) Stephen Fish winning the 15 Mile Seniors' event in 1970.

leading from the top

For the first time, this year's race marks the unique occasion of the current President, and two previous Presidents walking in the same race.

Tom Tidy, President

My earliest recollections of the Easter Monday 15 miles race date from the early 1930's, when as youngsters a group of us used to walk from Small Dole to Horton Corner each year and watch from the hillside.
In 1956 I escorted Sam Ring and as a result decided to enter the race in 1957 aged 31, and continued each year until 1977, but as the result of an accident I had to miss 1978-80.
However, with the help of Charlie Bean I again raced in 1981 and have continued each year to date, having completed 40 events.
In the 1960's and 70's I enjoyed many training walks over the downs accompanied and encouraged by John Henderson and this enabled me to complete 20 London to Brighton, 20 Hastings to Brighton, 3 London to Brighton and back, and 3 other 100 mile events.
My racing days finished at the end of 1977 and since then I have enjoyed just being a 'back marker'. Why do I still take part? It's because of the many friends I have made in Race Walking over the years and the enjoyment of taking part.

Len Warner

As a past President of the Club, I decided at the beginning of the year to attempt the 15mile walk subject to surviving the Sunday morning training sessions. So far so good, despite aching thighs and sore feet. I will be walking to raise sponsorship for the Georgemill Trust which is a local organisation, having just achieved charitable status to provide a nursing home in Steyning for the benefit of the residents in the Steyning area. I hope you will sponsor my walk. The Club encourages the younger members of the area to participate in a healthy pastime and I am proud and happy to be a 'Trustee of the Club'

Mike Blackie

The Athletic Club has for many years been an integral part of the Steyning community and I am very proud to have been its President for the period from 1995 to 1999.
I competed in this race over 30 years ago and I remember I felt fine until I reached Partridge Green when my legs started to cease up.
I struggled through Henfield-Small Dole-Beeding-Bramber crawling up Clays Hill only to find when I finally arrived at the Clock Tower everyone had gone home, apart from the St John Ambulance.
As this is the Millennium year, I decided to enter the 15 mile as a member of a relay team.
I have been training over the last few weeks, suffering from aches and pains, but it will have all been worth it if I can finish my part of the relay in a reasonable time

The Club Presidents in the Easter Monday 15 Mile event, Millennium Year 2000, with their own stories (or excuses – including incorrect wording – detail taken from the annual race brochure that year!).

J. F. L. (Johnny) Henderson
(Centurion) (see Chapter 6).
First 15 Mile Race 1927.
inner 1929, 1932 – 1936, and 1947.
Final Race 1977.

The legendary "Johnny" Miller.
First Seniors' Race 1957, last race 1998.
He never won the 15 Mile Race.

SOME OF THE 15 MILE EVENT PERSONALITIES

Norman Read
(Olympic Champion 1956)
Winner 1949 – 1951 and 1958.

Dennis Read,
Winner 1957, 1959 – 1963,
1965 – 1968, 1971.
First competed 15 Miles in 1957
(previously Raced as a Junior).
Still Race Walking.

Ernie Adcock
Winner 1912, held fastest time record until 1929 and last competed 1931:

George "Carrots" Holden
Winner, 1920, 1921, 1923, and 1925. Last raced in 1929

A. B. Grigg,
started Race Walking 1932. Last raced 1959. Never won.

rrell Stone
tional and International
nours, has the most wins in the
Mile Race, 13 in all. 1986 – 1988,
0 – 1994, 1996 – 1997, 1999
1 2002 – 2003. First competed as
oy, aged 9.

Dave Stevens
Competed at both National and
International levels. Senior
Race 1968, still race walking.
Winner 15 Miles 1973 – 1976.
Additionally, Dave has been a
stalwart in Steyning Walking
Club administration.

Graham Morris
(first raced as a 7 year old
boy in 1965, National
Boys' Champion 1972).
Represented Great Britain
in 1976, 1977 and 1981
Easter Monday 15 Mile
winner 1978 – 1984.
First man to achieve a win
in under two hours 1978.

reth Brown
nes winner of 15 Mile Easter Monday Races 1989, 2000, and 2001. Also, Junior
rnational, first competed in 15 Mile Easter Monday Walk 1988. Still race walking.

Charlie Bean
First 15 Mile Race 1958.
Still race walking.

This chapter would not be complete without the inclusion of the Read brothers, Norman, Brian, and Dennis. The life story of the most successful of this trio, namely Norman, is chronicled in many publications including the local history sourcebook including "A Steyning Connection" (published 2001) by this author. This work provides the fascinating detail of the extraordinary success story, leading to the highest honours achievable in sport, of this dedicated walker. The now legendary Johnny Henderson helped him, by high class and well thought out training routines, straightforward, honest encouragement and a shoulder to lean on with any troubles. Johnny himself, as has been stated in these pages, was a virtual certain Olympic candidate for the Olympic Games that would have taken place but for World War Two, and Norman Read went on to perform exactly that task. A Gold Medal in the Melbourne Games of 1956 was, and still is, an incredible success – the foundation of which was to be found in the road crunching practice walks in and around Steyning. Norman's accolade at the high pinnacle of sport by taking the Gold Medal, in a truly strong international field, albeit in New Zealand colours (for technical reasons) remains a talking point in the town today nearly fifty years on. It represents one special link between the athlete, Norman, and the town of his boyhood and upbringing – the very focal point of connection that is the underlying purpose of this book.

Into the bargain, (in addition to numerous county and higher honours) Norman left his stamp on the 15 Mile Steyning Easter Monday Races by taking first place in 1949, 1950, and 1951, to return in 1958 again with, barring two seconds, a record time of nearly under the two hours. Norman just had that extra something. It took another twenty years for the two hour limit to be smashed – by Graham Morris (now an official at the Races) in 1978.

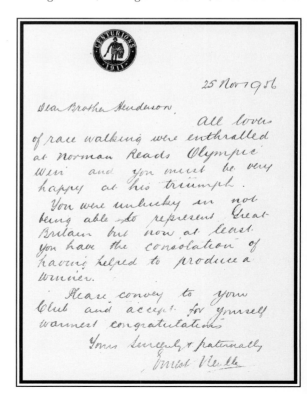

Dennis Read, the youngest brother, whilst not reaching to the highest point as his elder brother, nevertheless has a supreme record in the Steyning 15 Mile event (and indeed in other county and national competitions) by winning the event, firstly in 1957, again in 1959 to 1963, 1965 – 1968, and 1971, in all eleven outright victories. A feat only equalled by Darrell Stone in the 2002 race, and surpassed by him again in 2003.

Dennis started as a very successful walker (previously winning the Steyning Boys' races 1949 and 1950, and Southern Youth Champion in 1956) and won the 15 mile event on his first appearance. Dennis additionally secured his 1959 15 mile victory in the afternoon, whilst winning the morning Junior and Men's 7 mile event from the Clock Tower to the Kozi-Café on the Shoreham Road. Dennis still race walks today.

A reproduction of the letter from Ernest Neville, Vice President of the "Centurions", giving congratulations on Norman Read's 1956 Olympic success, to Club Secretary Johnny Henderson (note Centurion's refer to each other officially as "Brother"). Henderson as referred to in Chapter Six, who narrowly missed Olympic selection himself in 1936, helped to train Norman Read.

Brian, the remaining middle Read brother, also made his mark by regularly walking in the 15 mile event, his best position achieved being 5th. However, Brian did win both the Junior (Rising Sun course) Race in 1950 and 1951.

Traditionally, over the years, Steyning's walkers have gone on to participate in national and international events, to underpin Steyning Athletic Club's claim to be the senior Walking Club in the United Kingdom.

The list below is taken from a publication dated 1981 – even more honours followed for subsequent years.

Here are some of the outstanding achievements of members of Steyning A.C. since foundation in 1951.

Olympic Gold Medal 50 kms. Walk
Norman Read.   Melbourne, 1956.

Great Britain Internationals
Graham Morris
Tony Geal

Great Britain "B" International
Dave Stevens

Great Britain Junior Internationals
Steve Fish
Graham Morris

Race Walking Association Championships
S. Fish, National Youths, 1960.
G. Morris, National Boys, 1972.
C. Pope, National Boys, 1974 and 1975.
G. Brown, National Colts, 1980.
S. Brown, National Junior Girls, 1978.
S. Brown, National Intermediate Women, 1980.
H. Ringshaw, National Junior Girls, 1978 and 1979.

Inevitably, the final "Record Breaker" mentioned in this book, is Darrell Stone, the current 15 mile champion. The number of Darrell's victories in this Easter Monday event is an unequalled thirteen wins. His time in 1988, of 1 hour 47 minutes 19 seconds is still the course record today (2003).

Darrell relates, in the extract below, how he started Race Walking, the demands of the competition and the pressures and feelings of simply being in "The Race". Once more the link is forged between the 15 Mile Race, fellow competitors, both local and more recently, "guests", and the local community.

"Secretary, Dave Stevens' wife, Rose, was the start of it – the idea of trying race walking, which was to change my life forever – and a trip to the training evenings run by Johnny Henderson which sealed my fate. What seemed like endless figures of eight around the chairs laid out at each end of the Clubhouse created the beginnings of a 'technique' that Johnny would analyse like an old 'pro'. We were just 7 to 11 year olds, trying out this curious sport of Race walking, and had no concept of Johnny's walking career, but entrusted ourselves to his wise words and his constant reminder of "style first and the speed will come". How right he was to be! My first Easter Monday walks experience was in 1977 and Steyning High Street seemed as if a carnival had come to town. Everyone wanted to be part of it. At 9 years of age, the mile and a bit course was a major demand, but adrenaline kept most

of the 100 boys going, and when I examined the result sheet later in the day, coming 3rd in the 9 year olds seemed a very satisfactory return for my efforts.

A year later, in 1978, a few weeks before the race, training started again in the clubhouse mixed in with the usual assortment of Steyning Strikers footballers and school runners. Darren Smith was the target as he had come 2nd in my age group whilst the winner, Grant Ringshaw, simply seemed to be of professional status! I tried my best in that year, only to find that 3rd in my age group seemed to have my name on it again … but a year later, I was more determined than ever that this other boy would not demote me to the 'depths' of 3rd. In my final short course race in 1979, I managed to battle my way to 14th overall and 2nd in my age group, despite the fact that Darren tried his hardest to get back past me. The above sums up what Easter Monday meant, even in the early days when I had no chance of coming in the leading few, and personal battles were what made the day exciting. The banners, the parents screaming their support, it was all great fun, so exciting – and very serious.

Years later, I remember the fact that although some were competing at National level and even International level, most would find Easter Monday in Steyning the main nerve-racking race of the year, where local pride and passion were at a premium and a poor result would overspill into having a lack of enthusiasm for the Annual Easter Barn Dance at Jarvis Hall. I never won a race until I attempted the 15 miles as an 18 year old, but I do remember my breakthrough race as if it were yesterday. I was 16 and had to take on the likes of Donald Bearman (two years older and going for the course record), Gareth Brown (a multi-winner in the younger age groups), and Grant Ringshaw (who walked, ran and played football for Sussex). What a group to have grown up with, each one had talent to spare and they had put their mark on U.K. walking, not just on a local level. When I broke clear of Grant and Gareth, still in the wake of Donald, my world changed, as I realised that I could take on and beat the 'professionals' of my age. They were human after all; I was not just another athlete making up the numbers – and I finished 2nd. How different it had been when I did my first 'Beeding and back' walk as a 12 year old.

Nerves can turn your stomach upside down as many found out to their cost when first attempting this event. No other race can take your nerves to the level that Easter Monday does. Pressure is what you put upon yourself and so it was, in 1990, when I set the record that still stands today. I wanted to set a tough mark having already broken the previous record set by Graham Morris. Graham had re-written the record books for Easter when bringing the record down well below 2 hours and consistently doing so. It was his marks that I had to look to surpass. I had set up my stall in the first half of the race to 'The Bull' [Public House at Mockbridge, Henfield] and a time of 52 and a half minutes for the first half meant that I was fully committed and it would end in a fantastic record or disaster. However, I was so strong that day and never slowed as I powered to the finish. Some days, it just all fits into place, as a 20 year old, I set 1 hour 47 minutes, and 19 seconds – a time that shocked many and even impressed Norman Read when I saw him months later. Norman was the most successful walker Steyning Athletic Club can boast and despite missing the 2 hour mark by so little years earlier, Norman was my idol - Olympic Gold and Commonwealth Bronze, and such a gentleman. Norman was living proof that it could be done – from humble beginnings to achieving the ultimate sporting prize in his event. I hope that today's youngsters attempting the races each year realise how much they can achieve if they continue, persevere and excel.

Easter Monday is a race full of surprises, as local pride comes to the fore. Even when I had won several 15 miles and was expected to win again, guests were introduced and the inclusion of a talented guest from another club would instil fear that although I may *be the first local finisher, all would somehow be lost if a 'foreigner' was first up the High Street. The toughest Easter battle I ever had was in 2003, having let training slip a little after unsuccessfully trying to make the Commonwealth team in 2002 due to work commitments, beating my efforts to get into shape. Nevertheless, I decided that, as it was the 100th Easter Anniversary walks, I had to make every effort to put in my best possible performance. I trained to cover the 15 miles in around the 2 hour mark and took the attitude that it would be the best I could offer. I took the lead early on to ensure a genuine race, Gareth settled in on my shoulder, and the miles seemed to take forever with me testing my regular training partner over the years as best I could. When I sensed him weaken as I entered Upper Beeding, it was like a starter's pistol going off and memory took over for a mile, by which time, I had established a winning lead which remained 'till the finish. Even after all the years, it meant as much as the past triumphs.*

Upper Beeding High Street has always been the most eventful place. One year, a guest by the name of Steve Hollier (4th in the Commonwealth 50 km 1998) had decided to challenge me, but had not reckoned on the size of the little humpback bridge at the Bridge Inn [Public House, Bramber Bridge]. That little rise caused his legs to buckle and I nursed him home, as he was a 'guest' and no longer a threat after that.

Another time, it was a cool but sunny day and a vest and shorts was all that was required, but by the Kings Head [Public House, Upper Beeding] hailstones were piling down out of the grey stormy skies, and I remember my mother hanging out of the back of our old Mercedes with an umbrella over me trying to protect me as best she could from the worst the weather could offer. I would have laughed about it at the time, but the hail was stinging my shoulders as it bounced off them and I wondered what had lured me into such a demanding sport.

Why did I participate in this challenging race – one in which you needed stamina, strength, speed, technique, absolute commitment and time – more time that anyone could offer when fully working! But that was just it – if it had been easy, it would have been boring, and just to add to the equation was the constant abuse offered by young girls, boys, and passers by. Who in their right mind would do it?

Nevertheless, I loved it – Easter Monday was the start – the club was a family and a way of life. My personal passion was fulfilled by trips away at weekends in minibuses in search of success. This was amateur athletics at its best with no monies offered even as the level of the events got more serious.

I have competed in many countries and at the highest level for my country, but Easter Monday's Steyning walks encapsulate all that is healthy in sport from the youngest child in their first event to the international athletes, to the seniors of the event who remember far more Easters than I could imagine. That is what sport should still be about, and experiencing both the highs and lows of Easter Monday have left their mark on me forever."

Author's note: I also know what it is like to walk this 15¼ mile race; I have done it – in my late 50's and have great respect and admiration for anyone who puts themselves through such a public test of doggedness and stamina.

My apologies for any other "Record Breaker" who is at a loss to find that their story and picture is not included.

You are appreciated and whatever you have achieved has been recorded and will always be personal to you.

The limitation of space has imposed its unrelenting hand here – but a big "well done" from the entire production team, Vernon Books Ltd., and of course the author.

Ian Ivatt.
2003.

APPENDIX 1 – PAST PRESIDENTS OF WALKING RACES

President November 2003 – Ian Ivatt.

Tom Tidy, Esq.

Mrs. Betty Ash

Michael Blackie, Esq.

L. F. T. Warner, Esq.

J. F. Mackley, Esq.

J. Armour-Milne, Esq.

E. A. Parrott

Captain A. G. Smalley, D.S.C., RN.

Mrs. Marjorie Dingemans

Alexander Howard, Esq.

H.E.V. Bennett, Esq., M.B.E.

John Goring, Esq., C.B.E., T.D., D.L.

Lewis S. Wood, Esq.

Mrs. M. Purchas

W. F. Dewdney, Esq.

F. B. Purchas, Esq.

His Honour Judge Block D.S.C., D.L., J.P.

Dr. A. Dyce Davidson, O.B.E., T.D.

Admiral Sir Charles Little, G.C.B., G.B.E.

The Hon. Mrs. M. C. Hamilton-Russell

G. H. Recknell, Esq.

P. W. Felton, Esq.

R. Bateman, Esq.

F. Stubbings, Esq.

Dr. G. A. Dingemans

W. H. How, Esq.

Brigadier W. R. F. Osmond, C.B.E.

W. Leslie Burt, Esq.

The Hon. Sir Arthur Howard K.B.E., C.V.O., D.L., J.P.

Captain F. Purchas

John Goring, Esq., J.P.

Frank Duke, Esq.

Bertram Nicholls, Esq., P.R.B.A.

G. T. Breach, Esq.

Dr. C. W. Wheeler-Bennett

H. J. Burt, Esq.

Col. E. J. Suckling

Major L. College

G. Angus, Esq.

APPENDIX 2

MEMORABLE PHOTOS

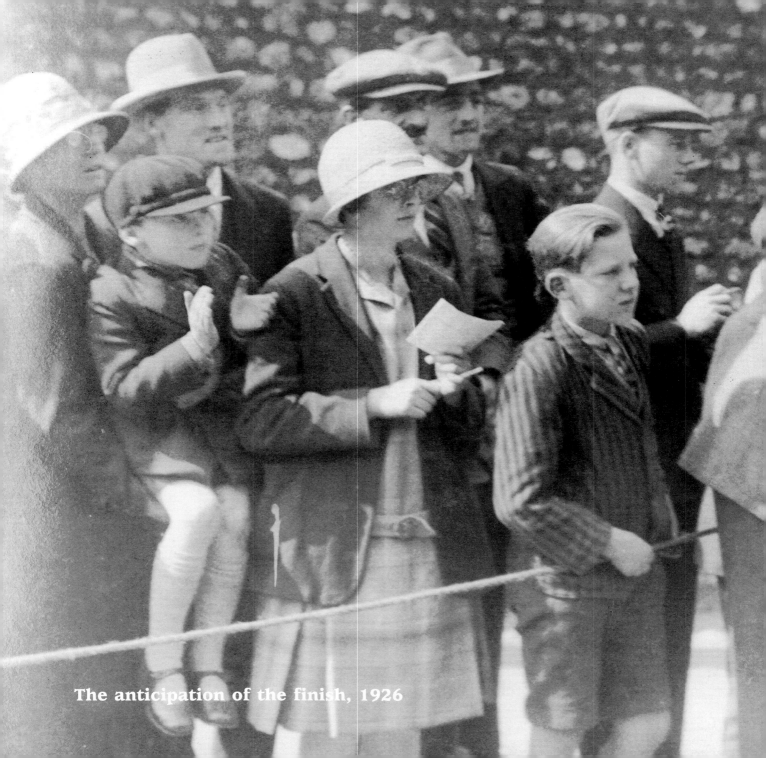

The anticipation of the finish, 1926

A club traing session

Lest we forget; the 1904 start in Church street, Steyning - note the walkers sporting caps.

Nearing the finish, 1904, with accompanying bicycles and cattle.
Judging by the time on the town clock the walker is not the first home.